COPYRIGHT © 2021 MANSAL DENTON

All rights reserved. No part of this publication may be reproduced, distributed, or transmitted in any form or by any means, including photocopying, recording, or other electronic or mechanical methods, without the prior written permission of the publisher, except in the case of brief quotations embodied in critical reviews and certain other noncommercial uses permitted by copyright law.

SACRED HUNTING
Rekindling an Ancient Spiritual Practice

ISBN   978-1-7377816-1-5

SACRED HUNTING

REKINDLING AN ANCIENT SPIRITUAL PRACTICE

MANSAL DENTON

TABLE OF CONTENTS

Foreword   1
Introduction   7

CALL TO ADVENTURE   15
   Seeking   17
   Rite of Passage   23
   Initiation   27
   Plant Teachers   31

INTENTIONS   35
   Charisma   37
   The Sacred Pact   41

PREPARATION   45
   Skill   47
   Sacrifice   51
   Humbling   55
   Ceremony   59
   Earth as Relative   63

MENTORSHIP   67
   Walking Among the Stars   69
   Quanah Parker   75
   Sacred Feminine   83

PURSUIT — 89

WHERE THE PATH LEADS — 91
Active Patience — 93
Loneliness — 99

MITAKUYE OYASIN: ALL ARE RELATED — 103
Permission — 105
Coherence — 109
Predators — 113

STALKING — 119
Oneness — 121
Surrender — 125

THE SHOT — 129
Volition — 131
The Right Shot — 137

THE MISS — 141
Shame — 143
Earth Time — 147
Sharing the Burden — 151
Guilt — 155

THE KILL **159**
   Violence 161
   Pain 167
   Responsibility 171
   Trauma 177
   Crossing Over 181

HONORING THE DEAD **187**
   Intimacy 189
   No Waste 193
   Return 199

FOR THE COLLECTIVE **203**
   Service 205
   Defend the Sacred 209

FOREWORD

WHEN MANSAL DENTON ENGAGED ME AS AN ELDER, AND we began monthly walks through the Texas Hill Country, little did I know what might unfold. We had begun our relationship when, in a cordial but limited exchange, he visited our sweat lodge ceremonies.

After a considerable hiatus that included trans-ordinary experiences in a prison term and with plant ceremonies in various settings, he requested that we begin our medicine walks again. By medicine, I mean the healing power of connecting through physical movement in a dimension of Nature less influenced by human culture. Soon in our purposeful wandering, Mansal shared a fascinating encounter stimulated by one of his trans-ordinary consciousness moments— a call to learn about and practice hunting in a primordial manner.

This significant book emerges a description of the manifestation of his vision of sacred hunting, sent from a hidden domain and set in the context of his moving personal narrative.

Such medicine walks often lead to larger forms of consciousness for both mentor and mentee. Slowly, in the process as mentor, I sensed a retrieval of a sub-self in my inner council of selves that lived next to my essence—the archetypal hunter.

This particular soul retrieval continues to enrich me and may offer that possibility for you. Briefly, let's see how it happened.

As Mansal and I explored his plant-induced visions and early hunting excursions, I encountered, in my own dreams, a pre-school boy peeking out from behind the shadows, one who lived through WWII. A tiny version of myself. The early 1940s constituted a time on the Llano Estacado of Texas, where I grew up, when the war created many shortages that included scarce protein. My father was an avid hunter, and he joined with a hunting band of locals to secure meat for our kitchen table.

A short drive from our family land lay the rich hunting grounds of the Comanche Chief, Quanah Parker, who had completed his Earth walk about the time of my father's birth. This great hunter's energy was still freshly embedded in the landscape, and he became my boyhood inspiration. Quanah shows up time and again, including at a significant moment in this book.

Leaving before sunrise on our hunts, we often drove a short distance to the tiny village of Quitaque, a Comanche word for buffalo chip. About three miles south of the sleepy store where we would stop for a rare soda, we parked our pickup trucks and headed west up a flowing creek called Los Lingos.

Tracking quail, both bobwhites and blue, we descended into a canyon via a fifty yard sandstone labyrinth, itself about twenty feet deep and, in most places, no wider than my father's shoulders. Scary and exciting. It wasn't unusual for us to encounter diamondback rattlesnakes as we moved through the distinctive smell of local sage that I would later learn to use in ceremony.

Many times we hunted in such remote canyons. By the time I was nine, my father gifted me with a .410 pump-action shotgun. It had a small chamber and twin bead sights to assist with accuracy, and an ambidextrous, thumb-operated safety to prevent accidents. At that early age, I struggled to carry it. Even though the kick threw about half the payload of a 12 gauge, it still sometimes knocked me on my rear end if I didn't plant myself solidly on the red dirt. In my adult life, I have opposed the widespread use of guns in society, but a respectful relationship with my .410 holds a special place in my heart these days.

When I left the Llano Estacado for graduate education, I left behind my .410 and my inner hunter. I don't know why.

Perhaps because our industrial educational process splits us off from both our primal souls and our food sources.

Such an experience of the sacred hunter being ignored by my mainstream, unaware ego resulted eventually in ignorance about the food chain. Mansal explores the importance of respectful connection not only with what we eat, but how we obtain what we eat through our energetic links with hunting for our food.

So it was that walking four or five miles one outing with Mansal facilitated the retrieval of my inner hunter, for whom I have affection as I write. That doesn't mean that I hunt these days. I don't. Even though I eat what Mansal and others in our community bring me from their hunting and fishing, I am not inclined to pull the trigger any more. As an octogenarian, I depend on younger hunters in the Earthtribe, our spiritual community, to bring me an occasional meal respectfully secured in the sacred manner described in this book.

My aspiration for you, the reader, is that your interior hunter will be more fully awakened. Whether your hunter is partially or completely obscured by a civilization bent on splitting us off from the Wild Heart of Nature will govern some of the reading. In both cases, the aim is the same: to return to the ancient connection with the Natural Order. Engage a larger version of yourself. There are many other features of Sacred Hunting that will enliven you and open doors of possibility, but the most important one for me was this recovery of the archetypal hunter. Embracing such a hidden self reaches back through the millennia and invites us all to recognize its value and wisdom as we cross a bridge into Earth's New Era.

Will Taegel
Wimberley, Texas
June 2021

INTRODUCTION

I HAD SPENT HOURS OF BOREDOM IN AMBUSH. NOW, A YOUNG, white-tailed deer slowly sauntered into my field of vision from the right. She was alone, a rarity, since I had encountered only herds earlier in the expedition. Moving slowly while eating, she walked into a position where I could shoot her, but nothing is guaranteed, even when things seem to be in my favor.

As if by instinct, she turned around and looked for something she had either heard or smelled that might prove as a warning for her to flee. She must have felt it was nothing worthwhile, for she continued choosing her steps gently but confidently in the same direction. My heart was thumping. Once she was close enough, I drew back the bow and waited.

The draw is eighty pounds and holding it too long presents a physical challenge. I held the heavy load steady. My muscles were being worked, and my heart beat faster in my chest as the blood pumped fervently into my arms while I struggled to remain as still as I could. My triceps began to cramp after a couple minutes in this position, but I was committed to my course.

When I let loose the arrow, the deer quickly dropped, but something wasn't right. I had injured but not killed a deer once before, and I instantly recognized the signs. I grabbed my knife and ran up to her to finish the job.

"Everything's going to be okay…You're doing great…Everything's going to be okay…" were the last words I whispered to her as I put a knife beneath her shoulder and into her heart. Her mouth opened; her legs kicked; she bleated in distress.

Her insides were so warm I felt her aliveness on my left hand, where the knife's end had met her fur. With my right hand, I held and caressed her head. She looked up at me with fear. I stayed alert, looking into her eyes, so she would not die alone.

I sat with her dead body in my arms for some time, staring at her, curious about the life she once had and her transition into death. There's an incredible presence in the silence that accompanies an animal's death. Time stops. For a few fleeting minutes, any doubts, troubles, or pain, past or future, I might have ceased to exist.

These words, as I write them, bring the experience to life once more. My stomach slightly sinks, and my hands become clammy. The deer is forever tattooed in my psyche, where she has a special place.

The act of taking a life is intimate. To kill another sentient creature, cutting away and consuming its flesh, making it part of my body, is perhaps the most intimate act of all. The animal is now part of my being, its soul merged with my own.

Hunting is my spiritual practice, the gateway and path into a deeper intimacy with Earth. It's a contemplation of my strengths and inadequacies as a man, reflecting how I show up in the world. It's a meditation on the impact my existence has and the death that accompanies every day of my grateful life. It's a portal that connects others, those I guide, with confidence, solidity, and responsibility. Above all, hunting has been where I've found my greatest healing.

By this I mean healing the emotional pain of the hardships in life that wound our spirit, heart, and soul. These leave lasting impressions on our character, worldview, and action. No matter how blessed our upbringing, everyone has these wounds that need mending.

For me, the greatest healing comes as a nurturing and unconditionally loving feminine presence. The reason we call her Mother Earth is because of this nourishing maternal energy.

When I first began hunting, I was in a relationship with a woman who was trying her best, but I felt neglected, underappreciated, and unloved. To cope with this pain, I turned to the Earth without at first knowing why.

I also found healing by becoming more confident and capable in my hunting practice. To know I could provide food for myself and others with my bare hands is emotionally restorative as well as pragmatic.

To rob a man of this basic ability is like raising a child without teaching it to read and write. Western civilization does a poor job preparing boys for manhood, imparting the skills and confidence they need. Hunting is the teacher of masculinity I never had growing up.

Feeling interconnected with all living things has also been healing. Many of society's ills, such as anxiety and depression, stem from a lack of connection—with oneself, those around us, our communities, and the planet.

Our relationship with and feeling of connection to the Earth have been indispensable throughout history. The word "indigenous" means "produced, growing, living, or occurring natively or naturally in a particular region or environment." Indigenous people are inextricably connected to a specific place on Earth, its dirt, grass, and plants.

The embodied practice of hunting is the core of my spiritual practice and connection to Earth, but a variety of other practices and guides also contribute to my healing.

In indigenous cultures, the elder is a fundamental source of inspiration and wisdom. The knowledge and information we're inundated with are easy to come by. Wisdom is not. It's transferred from an elder to an apprentice. I've been blessed to have a relationship with a man named Will Taegel or Star Heart, who has been my mentor and spiritual teacher since I was twenty-three.

Another practice is the use of entheogens, a term meaning "god within" used to describe plants that evoke non-ordinary states of consciousness for spiritual learning. Nearly all indigenous people used these substances for medicinal and religious purposes.

Hunting has always been vital for indigenous people. It's no wonder that entheogens have long been used for "hunting magic."

I'm also led by a firm commitment to and connection with my higher power. The terms *God*, *Universe*, *Great Spirit*, and *Sacred Mystery* all have connotations that are hard to parse or adequately describe this unique relationship. My higher power is an eco-spiritualism where animals, plants, and places are a connecting and unifying force. This is an animism I've made uniquely mine.

This book is a pathway reflecting the hunts I have experienced myself and facilitated for other men.

That pathway starts with a call to adventure. There is a primal yearning to hunt, to remember what our ancestors did and how they did it. This call is the voice in your mind that compels you to pick this book up in the first place. It's the inner voice guiding you towards a practice you may have no experience of or even feel uncomfortable with.

The next step involves the discernment and reflection needed to determine what and how you will hunt. The path continues through various practices and preparations, as well as the humbling required to become proficient in these new skills. We'll then follow the stalk, participate in the shot, honor the dead, and share the dead animal's flesh in service to friends and community.

The hunt you'll follow in this book has many diversions and byways. It amalgamates my own hunting stories—the stories of men whom I've mentored in my Sacred Hunting programs, and my hero's journey in awakening from a sad, hurt, and insecure boy in prison into the somewhat wiser man writing this book.

I hope I can express the wisdom I have gleaned from hunting and life, for your benefit. More significantly, I hope my words will stimulate action. The healing that arises from this path comes from the practice of hunting itself rather than reading about it.

I hope this book will inspire you to commit yourself to your healing and growth, and to becoming a hunter and active participant in nature.

CALL TO ADVENTURE

SEEKING

My hunt, you see, actually has little to do with elk. I knew that before I came. There is something else I am after, out here in the wild. I am searching for an even more elusive prey...something that can only be found through the help of wilderness. I am looking for my heart.

—JOHN ELDREDGE

WITH THE SUN STILL SHINING BRIGHT AND HIGH IN THE sky, I packed my compound bow, arrows, and a bag full of clothing. In camouflage pants and top, I prepared a box full of meat and a small portion of vegetables. This routine started at 3:00 p.m. on most weekdays during November, when nightfall comes around 5:30 p.m. in the Texas Hill Country.

This practice meant that I lost several hours of work and play every day. It was ostensibly to enable me to kill my first white-tail deer of the season and replenish my freezer with meat, which was getting dangerously low.

In retrospect, I realize what I was seeking from those days of hunting was not what I thought. Spending time in a noble pursuit amid the silence of fall, I was trying to find part of my heart in a faltering relationship.

A little over a month after this intense bout of hunting, she and I separated after four years together. What I was seeking in the woods was as much about solace and nurturance from Earth as meat to fill my belly.

My greatest fear and deepest wound is abandonment. In my tumultuous, formative, early years, I, an only child, struggled against entanglement with my mother in a house my alcoholic father ran tyrannically.

Although my relationship with my father has mended, some of my earliest memories were of running away from home with my mother when he was in an alcoholic stupor, or of sitting in the emergency room when his rage accidentally sent my mother there.

I brought this baggage and the wound of abandonment into my first, long-term relationship at the age of twenty-five. This led to codependent patterns not conducive to a healthy, long-term partnership, although they did help us both grow. We separated four times in all, for varying periods, all of which caused further rifts and fissures.

Her wounding meshed imperfectly with my own. Her parents' divorce early in her childhood and a steady rotation of stepparents understandably led to a pattern of attachment-avoidance. Becoming too close to someone led inevitably to pain, which caused her to pull away. My own wounding saw that as a cue to pull her closer. It was a tug of war that made neither of us happy but opened me to the greatest compensation of my life: *hunting*.

As my relationship teetered at the end, I found myself drawn to hunt most nights of the week. I told myself I was doing it for the meat.

This is not the first time that I was guided to a spiritual pursuit such as hunting for a reason my ego could feel comfortable with, but deep down I was guided by intuitions I was unaware of.

When I first decided to hunt, I wanted to have a closer connection to my food. I wanted to feel what it was like to take the life of an animal and eat it, instead of buying meat from grocery stores and restaurants. Many men who go on hunts I facilitate feel the same way, and it's a great starting point.

But some part of my soul knew that hunting meant more than simply killing an animal for food. I couldn't put this into words then, and it took a long time to recognize that I was seeking something much wilder—what John Eldredge speaks about.

This is a truism that now pervades my life. I often seek an experience, relationship, or teaching that appears, on the surface, to have one purpose, but there's another, deeper motivation, inspiration, or endeavor that can only be seen with time and reflection.

My attitude is that it's worth listening to what I'm drawn towards. What I tell myself may not be the real reason I'm seeking it, and this gets me into trouble from time to time. My ego is as capable of sneaking motivation under my radar as my intuition and heart are, but when I'm surrounded by high-integrity friends who hold me accountable, this hidden motivation generally serves me well.

Following this voice is something new for me. In the past, I would rationalize almost everything and make decisions based on the money it cost or time it took. These are real considerations, but they don't allow deeper wisdom to come through.

A question my former partner asked was a turning point. Towards the end of a fifteen-mile hike in Glacier National Park, I shared my resistance to paying the substantial fee to attend a men's ayahuasca retreat I had been invited to. She asked me, "If we weren't together, would you go?" The answer was a resounding yes. I decided to follow that intuition, as opposed to my rational calculations, and I'm glad I did, since that decision changed my life.

I've realized the intuition behind my seeking only with experience. We feel more alive if we give ourselves permission to act on what we seek.

RITE OF PASSAGE

Unadorned suffering is the bedmate of masculine growth. Only by staying intimate with your personal suffering can you feel through it to its source...feel your suffering, rest with it, embrace it, make love with it. Feel your suffering so deeply and thoroughly that you penetrate it, and realize its fearful foundation.
—David Deida

EVERY MORNING AT 3:30 A.M., PRISON GUARDS WOULD enter my unit of fifty-four men and serve breakfast trays to the groggy, sleepwalking inmates. Depending on the guard's disposition, some would open the door and leave the trays for us to distribute among ourselves later on. Other guards would follow strict rules, forcing us all to wake up for the fifteen minutes it took to get a tray.

Nobody wanted to eat breakfast at 3:30 a.m., but some of us didn't feel we had a choice. We would gobble down what warm food there was and go back to sleep.

Prison is a uniquely disempowering experience. I had almost no sway there and didn't control when or what I ate or when I worked out. There is little I could control. This was one of the most humbling experiences of my life, and for that I'm incredibly grateful.

It took time and healing to arrive at that perspective, however. In what I believe to be my life's rock-bottom moment, I was lying curled up in a ball, covered with a flimsy prison blanket, trying to control a soulful cry that could not be dammed. Whimpering, sniffling, squeezing my core tightly, I did my best to avoid prisoners who might witness my pain.

I sat in prison because of immoral decisions I made between the ages of eighteen and twenty. Back then, I was an avid history fan interning in a small museum located in the garage of an elderly man in my hometown. I worked there to bolster my résumé and would spend time reading about past events I found compelling.

At the same time, I was connecting deeply with a woman who lived in Switzerland. We met online, discussing historical events. She spoke German, a language I became fluent in over two years to be able to speak with her. We connected on all the topics I thought no other beautiful woman would be fascinated by: history, classical music, and European culture.

After graduating high school, I wanted to be with her, which was a fair conclusion for a teenage boy who had never kissed a girl. When I told my parents my decision, their request was just as fair: if I was to live and go to school in Europe, I needed to pay my own way.

The museum internship, and the documents worth thousands of dollars housed there, were an easy target for a young boy deciding to take the easy way out. Due to my insecurities, shame, and the need to find an intimate partner, I stole the documents and sold them to pay to go to college in Europe for nearly two years.

The relationship ended tragically. When I returned to the United States to visit family for the holidays, the authorities were waiting. They needed more proof, which I unwittingly but gladly gave them. The day of my arrest, nearly twenty police cars, the district attorney, Texas rangers, and other assorted agents raided my home, looking for evidence against me.

My first arrest and night in jail, and the media publicity surrounding them, were a pivotal point in my life. It was my first experience, at age twenty, of real-world bitterness. As a privileged child untested by the world, I soon went into a deep depression.

Over the next four years, these challenges enabled me to grow stronger and take more responsibility for myself. I started meditation, read self-help books, and paid my own way *legally* through the University of Texas at Austin. At age twenty-three, I felt I had turned things around when the case came to a climax, and I was sentenced to eight years in prison.

I was stunned and shocked. My expectation was that I would avoid prison because I had "done well" after my initial arrest. My lawyer felt it was likely I would serve only ninety days.

The rock bottom moment, lying in my prison bunk crying, was precipitated by a letter from my lawyer. He acknowledged that he didn't know when I would get out, and I should learn to get comfortable where I was. To add to this stinging letdown, I learned my grandfather was likely to die of cancer before I could see him again.

It was all too much to bear.

In his book *Iron John,* poet Robert Bly, founder of what he describes as the "expressive men's movement," calls this "ashes." It's a scathing moment in life, a trial by combat.

The ego is diminished during this time, and prison certainly diminished mine.

Although I didn't know it then, the great thing about rock bottom is that there's only one way to go from there.

INITIATION

Everything can be taken from a man but one thing:
the last of the human freedoms—to choose one's
attitude in any given set of circumstances,
to choose one's own way.
—Viktor Frankl

IF THE FIRST THREE MONTHS OF MY EXPERIENCE IN PRISON were characterized by resistance, victimhood, and self-pity, sovereignty, self-responsibility, and empowerment defined the second half. After grieving the loss of my expectation of a quick release on my bunk, I was free to take full ownership for myself, my time, and my mind, regardless of my external circumstances.

It was in this phase of my experience that I dedicated myself to reading every self-improvement book in the prison library. I read Eckhart Tolle's *The Power of Now*, the ancient Hindu scripture *Ramayana*, and *Flow* by Mihaly Csikszentmihalyi. I read dozens of books rather than watch TV and movies mindlessly.

I worked out in prison daily, bodyweight-training to maintain fitness and strength. At one point, I attracted a host of prison admirers when I asked a small man nicknamed

"Cutthroat" if I could squat with him over my shoulders to provide extra weight. Suddenly, I went from a nerdy city-boy with glasses to "Professor" and "Doctor," uttered with respect for how I was choosing to eat healthy with the few options we had.

I had been given the gift of personal agency, understanding that, no matter my external circumstances, I could control my attitude as Victor Frankl had done to survive concentration camps during the Holocaust.

My experience in prison was a rite of passage, coming with all the lessons of a traditional trial-by-fire, such as humility, agency, courage, and determination.

Tyson Yunkaporta, an elder in the aboriginal Apalech clan, once told me that due to the poverty and cultural degradation of Australia's native people, prison has become a rite of passage for men there, too. It serves the purpose traditional rites of passage have played the world over and teaches boys to be humble and not place themselves over the collective good of those around them.

In aboriginal culture, the biggest sin is to place one's individual self above the collective or the land. Given how egalitarian indigenous people are, selfishness is a taboo often punishable by death, because the tribe cannot survive with selfish actors.

This goal of using rites of passage to humble boys is seen all over the world. The Pueblo from what is now the southwest USA isolated teenage boys in underground *kivas* for nine months. They were silent during which time, listening to the voices of the "second mother"—the Earth. The Mawé people of South America have boys as young as twelve wear a glove full of bullet ants.

Most of these rites of passage would be considered abuse today, but they served an important purpose for the tribe, just as prison served that role for me.

One of our society's most destructive cultural trends is the lack of guidance in the passage from boyhood into manhood. The suffering, challenges, and humility that rites of passage provide tribal cultures are much needed today but are absent.

Because hunting is so important to tribal cultures, it also plays a significant role in rites of passage. In many tribes, a boy does not become a man until he can successfully hunt. The ability to provide food for himself and the community marks the transition into manhood. Hunting can also be a most humbling experience, marrying the pragmatic rite of passage of providing food to the humbling rite of passage so important for masculine growth in traditional cultures.

For men in America and elsewhere in the West, who must navigate their own way into masculinity and create their own rites of passage, hunting is a cornerstone tradition. It is one of the core practices I utilize for my spiritual growth and the linchpin of the experiences I facilitate for other men.

I have created Sacred Hunting immersions and experiences to guide men through the rite of passage so critical to our sex and species. I facilitate these experiences for other men, because guidance, wisdom, and a rite of passage could have kept me from committing crimes and going to prison. Often, our greatest wounds become our most powerful gifts.

PLANT TEACHERS

THE MECHANICAL ADVANTAGE OF A COMPOUND BOW MAY make it easier to operate than a traditional one, but for a beginner, pulling back eighty pounds is still a challenge. As I nock my first arrow, pulling it back proves strangely unwieldy. I'd exercised the rhomboid muscles in my back, but not how the bow required. After a few shots, I felt more at ease with the bow and the fluidity needed for this new pattern of movement.

I've used a compound bow from the outset of my time hunting. I appreciated the romantic allure of hunting with a bow, but far more important was that, as a convicted felon, it's illegal for me to use a rifle. The bow-hunting learning curve is steep for a beginner, and, despite highly skilled coaches, the pressure of learning how to do it right loomed heavily.

I was in this place, not more than a month before my first hunting experience, when I participated in a men's ayahuasca retreat. Ayahuasca is a hallucinogenic brew, native to the Amazon basin, that indigenous people have used for thousands of years to evoke visions and healing. It is a strong "entheogen," an alkaloid compound that evokes a feeling of being connected to a higher power or divinity.

During the first night of the retreat, I was deeply under the force of the "medicine" when I saw in my mind's eye an image of the deer I would be hunting. The emotions overwhelmed me, and I began to cry, first as a few tears, then a deluge streaming down my face.

At that moment, and for the first time in my life, I asked God and the Universe to allow my arrow to penetrate the animal through the heart, killing it cleanly and quickly. I asked that the animal have a painless death. This was the beginning of my relationship with a higher power.

Two months later, just one month after my first hunt, I again sat in ceremony, in Mexico, newly obsessed with death. This place was in what indigenous people believed to be the home of Aztec deity, Quetzalcoatl, a powerfully sacred place if there ever was one. I wanted a connection with the animals whose death was required for me to eat. I needed a connection to the reality of the death that I will face with family members and with myself.

At one point during the ceremony, I sat on a rocking chair on a wooden porch, petting the spirit of the animal I had killed. The biggest takeaway from that experience was a commitment, when at home, only to eat meat and fish I have killed myself or with which I have a relationship.

Reading the book *The Body Keeps the Score*, I recognized how much trauma humans store in their bodies. I realized that if humans experience this, so do the animals we eat. If I was eating an animal full of trauma from factory farms, that trauma was literally becoming a part of me and my body, and I wanted nothing to do with that.

These and other entheogens have set the context for what hunting was and could be as a spiritual practice. I derived much of the philosophy I bring into Sacred Hunting experiences from the two ceremonies I've recounted, which sensitized me to both the gravity of taking an animal's life for food and how my body receives the meat.

The Dagara people of western Africa consider plants to be the most intelligent beings. Animals are second, and humans third. People of the tribe must go to the school of plants and animals to find their mission and place on Earth.

That's what I did. My experiences with plant teachers provided me context and guidance, and my experiences with hunting fostered a relationship to animals. Together, they have provided me with a purpose, the life's path I now walk.

Westerners, myself included, are so desensitized to the connection with plants that we often need entheogens to "get the message." Over time, I've recognized that plant teachers need not be mind-altering. The more deeply one relates with Earth, the more intimacy with a specific place and its unique flora develops, and the subtler the teachings.

INTENTIONS

CHARISMA

The only thing smarter than a coyote is God.
—Native American proverb

A HUNTER LOOKS ONTO A LANDSCAPE DIFFERENTLY THAN A non-hunter. In wide, expansive environments, I maintain a broad gaze, soaking up the "big picture." I see everything around me, but not very well defined or clearly. The objective is to spot subtle movements or shapes in this big picture that do not belong to the pattern.

Standing atop a small, rocky hill, I looked at the landscape in the twilight hour thirty minutes before sunset. Seeing movement in front of my small group of three men, I raised my binoculars to get a closer look, expecting to find prey that could be hunted.

Instead, there was the largest coyote I'd ever seen, with a big, bushy tail, trotting through the landscape. Only sixty or seventy yards from us, it was surprisingly unconcerned at our presence. It may have been on a mission, or we may have had the wind in our favor, or it somehow understood my intentions.

The feelings of awe and reverence that arise when I see a charismatic animal such as that coyote are difficult to express. I become a gleeful observer wondering what the coyote is doing and trying to learn about the species through the clarity of my binoculars.

Animals like the coyote become charismatic because of their personalities, which are perceptible to those who pay attention. They are curious, feel fear, and have an intelligence that we humans recognize, which brings them to life for us.

An animal's charisma, often related to how much they act or behave like humans, plays a big role in whether we decide to hunt them. A friend once shared a story of traveling all the way to the Brooks mountain range in remote northern Alaska, only to feel unable to kill a bear he encountered there. He recounted how he looked through the sights of his rifle and saw this bear chasing after a butterfly, serenely in his own world. At that moment, he couldn't shoot it.

Predators in particular remind us of ourselves. They have two eyes in front of their face. Bears sometimes stand on their two hind legs. This humanity often becomes overwhelming for those with empathy and an open heart.

The Navajo people have strong beliefs about charismatic predators. Those who killed a coyote were said to get "coyote illness," and a ceremony was required to return to harmony with the spirit of the animal.

The Maidu of modern-day California have a powerful myth about the coyote, which reflects the stark contrast to how modern hunters relate to the coyote, considering them vermin and a nuisance. Our feeling is often that we might as well kill them if there's no "use" for them. The Maidu didn't necessarily have a practical use for coyotes either, yet their story reflects the reverence that many people had for the animal, raising it to godlike status.

The Earth Maker is floating in water at the beginning of time when Coyote calls out to him. They sing together to create the world. When Earth Maker creates people, Coyote vows to introduce evil to the world. Earth Maker orders the people to destroy Coyote, but he uses supernatural trickster powers to outwit them. The myth ends with Earth Maker—God—recognizing that the Coyote's power is equal to his own. To some cultures, not even God was smarter than Coyote.

THE SACRED PACT

> *There is a story among the Lakota Sioux that the moon was once like the earth, but that the people up there stopped making sacred, and the energy of their world ran out. More important than our behavior or action is our intention.*
> —Randall Eaton

BEFORE ANGLO-EUROPEANS COLONIZED THE AMERICAS, IT was known as "Turtle Island." There were no animal trackers or stalkers among the Lakota people, who inhabited the North American Great Lakes and Ohio River Valley before being pushed to the plains of the present-day Dakotas, Montana, and Wyoming.

Before being colonized, the Lakota hunted differently. Each boy would prepare himself for his first hunt by working closely with his band's medicine man. In council, he would learn oral traditions and wisdom from these elders. He would enter the sweat lodge or *inipi*, which means "sacred place," and would also vision quest, spending four days alone in the wilderness without food, awaiting the Earth spirits and their messages.

All these activities were intended to bring energy and intention to his first hunt. When he was ready, the boy would go into the forest and sit down. During his spiritual training, he had connected with the animals and asked for and been granted permission to take the life of a deer. Now, the boy simply needed to have faith, and the deer would come to him. There was no need to trick the deer; they had a pact and relationship, and both fulfilled their end of the bargain.

In retrospect, this is similar to my first hunt. I participated in sweat lodges, held council with my spiritual teacher, and went to arguably the most sacred place that I'd found: ayahuasca ceremony. With tears streaming down my face, I asked for permission and guidance to take an animal's life.

My patience was tested as I sat in the same ambush for days on end. I saw numerous animals at dawn and dusk, but none of them were in the right position, nor did they speak to me like they did to the boys in the Lakota initiation.

Near the end, a small family of antelope came into view, jovial and playful. All females, the young were playing with one another, the aunts, mothers, sisters, all seeming upbeat and energetic. I wondered whether they would come and go as the animals had done earlier. Sitting patiently with my bow, I awaited a sign and opportunity.

Their joy and playfulness provided me the opportunity to draw back my bow, take aim, and fire. An animal jumped up and kicked its legs with shock and then ran. I was sure

I had hit her, but was not certain where until she fell to the ground. As I peered through my binoculars with a mixture of adrenaline-fueled pride and sadness, I could see the other antelope become curious.

Having run away, they returned to search for their friend, mother, or sister. They sniffed the body and looked around, trying to piece together what had happened. They left dejected, saddened, and with a completely different energy than they had come. I could feel the difference.

Once I had an opportunity to go to the animal and have a moment, I learned that the shot was perfectly through the heart. It was unheard of for a first-time hunter, especially with bow and arrow, to have such a perfect shot. It was a fulfillment of the sacred pact that I had created with that animal through spiritual preparation and asking for guidance.

Big game, such as elk, deer, and bison, were my first choices for hunting. These large animals provide bountiful meat, and all have special places in the hearts of the indigenous peoples of Turtle Island.

Smaller animals, like duck, pheasant, or rabbit, have less appeal to me. They're magnificent creatures in their own right, but the number of sentient lives I would have to take to sustain myself is too high. I would much rather kill a single bison and live from that over a year or two than kill two rabbits per day.

The Comanche, a tribe of the southern Texas plains, agreed. They only ate fish or birds if they were starving. But for many people, the thrill and fun of bird hunting draws them to this quarry rather than big game.

All these animals know that they are prey and understand the game they are playing in this circle of life. In contrast, predators like the coyote, wolf, or rattlesnake are to be revered and not killed. The way that I approach this moral question is to consider any animal that I will eat to be prey. If I cannot or will not eat it, then I will not kill it. This is part of the pact.

Being true to this pact requires discernment and brings intentionality to the hunting practice. These intentions are the foundation of the sacred, and the more intention that we bring into our hunting practice, the more sacred it becomes. The same is true in our daily lives.

PREPARATION

SKILL

Every man has a vocation to be someone: but he must understand clearly that in order to fulfill this vocation he can only be one person: himself.
—Thomas Merton

THE SKILLS TO BE GOOD HUNTERS AND WARRIORS CAME naturally to Comanche boys. When hunting skill dictates life and death, the human mind can do wondrous things. Boys were given their own horses at the age of four and were quickly expected to perform tricks, such as picking up items off the ground at a full gallop.

A grandfather or elderly male gave bows and blunt arrows to boys at age six. Within a few months, they were expected to go out with other boys and shoot birds. By the time a Comanche brave was an adult warrior, he could release twenty arrows in a matter of seconds with lethal accuracy and could fire up to ten arrows before the first hit the ground.

Few modern men have attained the incredible hunting skills that Comanche men acquired. I started with far more modest intentions and preparation, and to this day, I can only dream of the capabilities these men possessed.

As I've mentioned, my foray into archery began against my will. My desire to hunt was in tension with past events in my life. Because of my felony conviction, I couldn't use a rifle to hunt game, but a bow and arrow were legal.

Sitting in the ayahuasca ceremony and asking a higher power for assistance were only part of my quest. The responsibility of a successful hunt was developed in the daily practice of learning and perfecting archery. I was determined to hunt and kill ethically.

A compound bow is different from the traditional bows the Comanche would have used. It uses mechanics to make pulling back the string much easier. I hunt with an eighty-pound draw weight, which I would be unable to pull back if I were using a traditional bow. It still requires ample strength, especially in my back's rhomboid muscle.

Practicing daily, multiple times a day is imperative for becoming a good archer. Although it's possible to practice with thirty to fifty arrows at a given time, it's far better to mimic hunting itself, maintaining good form while shooting a few well-placed arrows throughout the day.

Archery is as much a mental game as a physical one. Many archers, myself included, use a checklist of items to ensure the greatest opportunity for success.

I start with the left-hand grip externally rotated for stability. When I pull back my bow, I look beyond the sight at the target. Once I have found my right hand's resting place toward the back of my cheek, I look through the peep sight, which is a rudimentary target, to line up my shot. When I feel ready, before I have waited too long, I place my finger on the trigger of the release, and, leading with my back muscles, squeeze with my entire arm.

I have been blessed with many great archery teachers, whom, as a first-time hunter, I desperately needed. Many of the practices used for accuracy in archery competitions do not work in hunting, when you might only have a couple of seconds to take a shot on a live animal.

You never stop learning archery skills. I've reached many plateaus, regressed, and needed support to get back to my best shooting.

Learning the rhythms of nature is another valuable preparation for the hunt. Almost all large prey are crepuscular, meaning they are most active at dawn and dusk. This is typically when the hunting is best, because animals are out moving, searching for food or mates. Animals are creatures of habit who frequently move in the same places at the same time of day.

You can understand where animals are moving by the trails they leave. Consistent walking over the same areas creates pathways in the grass, which are clues about where to set up an ambush. They might, for example, lead toward a small stream where animals drink.

To hunt ethically, one must ensure the cleanest and quickest chance of success. Despite the romanticism of hunting with a bow and arrow, it's not necessarily "the right way," as it's sometimes described. It's a big commitment and one that many people make without the follow-through required. Men who participate in Sacred Hunting experiences usually hone their rifle skills first.

My legal standing means I will be forever tethered to my archery practice if I am to hunt and kill the wild game that sustains me and the community. The commitment to developing my archery and general hunting skills has been extremely rewarding, but these skills are only one small piece of the preparation puzzle.

SACRIFICE

> *We believe it is up to every one of us to help each other, even through the pain of our bodies. Pain to us is not "abstract," but very real. We do not lay this burden onto our god, nor do we want to miss being face to face with the spirit power.*
> —John Lame Deer

RAINY SEASON ON THE BIG ISLAND OF HAWAII IS CONstantly wet and dreary. Sitting in my small, makeshift room on an inflatable mattress, my mind wanted movement, but my body did not.

For five days I had been in isolation in my room, eating 700 calories or less—no fat, no salt. I was feeling dizzy and lethargic. Underneath all of these practices was a process known as a *dieta*, connecting to a plant from the Peruvian jungle called chiric sanango.

The ancient process is to weaken the physical body and reduce distractions so as to be able to receive the plant's teachings and lessons. The chiric is used daily as the "teacher plant," the centerpiece of the plant diet providing unique healing and teaching. Ayahuasca is the "master plant" with particularly potent curative and spiritual powers.

The process is rigorous, and I learned a lot about myself doing it. To go through a *dieta* is to sacrifice time, physical well-being, energy, and the opportunity to do anything else in a nine-day period.

From the indigenous perspective, sacrifice is a major currency of gratitude and appreciation. *Dieta* is a commitment common to South American tribes, while fasting is one common to North American tribes.

I often go on three-day fasts before my hunting trips. The absence of food is a perfect way to acknowledge gratitude for Earth, which provides us abundance regardless of how we treat her.

During my fasting, I often sweat in a sauna or sweat lodge to amplify the experience. More discomfort, pain, and sacrifice, up to the edge of what I am capable of.

An animal will give its life for me to eat and live. To be in alignment with what I am asking of this animal and of the Earth, I must be willing to undergo a sacrifice of myself.

There are many forms of sacrifice, some more intense than I am prepared to commit to right now. The Sun Dance is an annual sacrifice in many Plains tribes that takes place over days of fasting from both food and water. It often includes repetitive dancing, and participants place hooks attached to a tall pole through their skin and dance until the hooks rip their flesh.

To many in the western world, this form of personal sacrifice may sound masochistic, but to John Lame Deer, a Lakota medicine man, pain and sacrifice are central to his culture:

> If we offer Wakan Tanka a horse, bags of tobacco, food for the poor, we'd be making him a present of something he already owns. Everything in nature has been created by the Great Spirit, is part of Him. It is only our own flesh which is a real sacrifice—a real giving of ourselves. How can we give anything less?

In the sacrifice, I am prostrating myself from a place of humility. My fasting, the *dieta*, the sweating, and abstinence from sex for a period are humbling acts intended to place me in right relationship with my higher power.

Sacrifice as a hunting practice comes in many shapes and forms. As any public-land elk hunter will tell you, traipsing through the mountains, hiking fifty or more miles in a week, is a form of physical sacrifice. Losing sleep to hunt is a sacrifice, as it takes time out of each day to practice archery.

There are many forms of sacrifice. For the old, indigenous ways, fasting, sweating, and abstinence are *spiritual* forms of sacrifice that provide a deeper layer of intentionality.

HUMBLING

*Men carry their superiority inside
and animals outside.*
—Russian proverb

FLAKY SHALE ROCKS SLIDE DOWN THE MOUNTAIN, tumbling and gaining momentum. There are no trees, as this steep, rocky place allows them no place to put roots down. There is a terrifyingly clear view to the bottom. As my guide and hunting mentor encourages me along, both the cameraman and I look at one another with some consternation.

In our quest for elk, we had ended up in unenviably dangerous terrain in the Sawtooth Mountains of central Idaho. Without much of an option, our best route was through rather than around the flaky shale rocks. For me, the hunt had stopped, for not only had the pursuit of game become unimportant, but my survival felt jeopardized.

When I characterize my relationship with heights, I like to say, "I'm not afraid, but I'm not comfortable either." But sometimes I am afraid, and this was one of those moments.

After ten or fifteen minutes gingerly crossing the side of the mountain, my emotions were running wild. For three days I had been hiking nearly ten miles a day, climbing hundreds of feet in elevation, with no pathways, bushwhacking through the mountains. We would start before dawn, come back to camp after dark, and then start filming for two to four hours, until it was time to sleep.

The rigor of mountain hiking, poor sleep, not eating: I was exhausted. The fear I experienced on the shale rocks was simply the catalyst sending me into a tailspin of anger, doubt, rage, confusion, and sadness. I questioned why I was on the mountain, what I was doing hunting elk in Idaho, why I was part of a documentary exploring society's relationship to death through the lens of hunting, and why I was in the intimate relationship I was in. I questioned everything and had answers for nothing.

When I got back to camp, the dam broke, and the tears flowed. To be so thoroughly humbled by nature and the mountains was a new experience. I had been humbled before, by prison, by entheogens like ayahuasca, and by people, but I had never been so thoroughly humbled by Earth herself.

There is a common thread of humility among hunters who have spent much time in nature. Whether they are sitting in a tree stand in the bitter cold winter or climbing dozens of miles in search of elk, the pursuit of animals in the old way humbles.

We live in a world that could use much more humility.

Tyson Yunkaporta, a man of aboriginal descent from the Apalech clan, told me that to the indigenous in Australia the original sin is placing oneself above the land or other people. In their origin myth, the troublemaker emu creates the story, "I am greater than you. You are less than me." Thus, the myth of the "special human" full of narcissism was born, and it's been the scourge of our civilization ever since.

For aboriginal men, a rite of passage from boyhood to manhood was intended to be a humbling experience showing that, without a shadow of a doubt, the individual boy was not special or worth more than the collective.

These experiences, as traumatic and brutal as they may seem, served a purpose. They were ritualized, ceremonial humility, much like I experience in the mountains, cold ponds, and mosquito-infested forests while hunting.

The painstaking labor of some hunting experiences is part of the process. What's more, many times I put in great effort without results.

It's one thing to practice rigorously for months, hike fifty miles in the mountains, and spend nine days to kill an elk and provide meat for the entire year. It's something altogether different to do all this and miss the kill with a shot poorly placed four inches to the left.

In the holy Hindu text, the *Bhagavad Gita*, the godlike figure Krishna tells his disciple Arjuna, "You have the right to your labor, but not to the fruits of your labor." In the end, all we have is doing the work. Success is not guaranteed is a truism that's been part of our species for a long time.

Even when successful, one may still be humbled. To carry an entire animal in addition to one's gear for miles is no small feat. I still remember the Mars-like landscape of Molokai island, Hawaii, trodding along with a seventy-pound axis deer on my back. My joints ached, and it felt like I could twist an ankle or blow out a knee at any moment. As tiresome as it was, this is nothing compared to more experienced hunters killing elk or moose ten or twenty miles deep in the wilderness, requiring many long trips to pack out.

When nature humbles me, I respect it more. In my pain, I realize that if the Earth wanted to break me, she could. This humility has often come up in my spiritual or mind-altering journeys, and the image that is conjured is me bowing, head on the ground, in deference to the planet. Before hunting, I had none of this.

CEREMONY

We do not go into ceremony to talk about God. We go into ceremony to talk with God.
—Quanah Parker

THE AOUDAD IS A SPECIES OF SHEEP NATIVE TO NORTHERN Africa, and imported to Texas to inhabit the rocky, arid, western portions of the state. With large, scythed horns, they roam the Texas Hill Country, often underappreciated in favor of native white-tailed and axis deer. In my early experiences hunting, the aoudad were consistently portrayed by established hunters as the dumb, inedible sheep that disrupt deer hunting. I learned quickly that aoudad were special creatures, tasted great, and were worthy of admiration and respect.

Nestled in a cove too small to call a cave, but large enough for four men to share shady space, we looked on as an aoudad mother and two babies came crashing into a canyon and continued running out of view. It was an incredible sight to see this animal in its element, sharing its gifts with us. It also punctuated what was, in the words of one participant, "the greatest journey of my life."

Ceremony comes in many forms. Sometimes it is in the form of an entheogen or hallucinogenic substance, such as ayahuasca, psilocybin mushrooms, or San Pedro cactus. Sometimes it is in the form of breathwork or burning incense, and sometimes all of the above.

Some ceremonies are more powerful than others owing to the substances involved and the setting. All of them provide value due to their intentionality.

Before I hunt personally or facilitate groups of men hunting, I burn cleansing herbs, sage, and palo santo. I say prayers and smudge, wafting smoke from these burning herbs over my bow and arrows. This brings intentionality to the weapons I'll be using to take another animal's life.

In these ceremonies I have the opportunity to remind my subconscious mind that I'm not on the land to take something from it to enrich my ego. I'm there as part of nature, partaking in an act that will feed me and serve the land and what is greater than myself.

The Huarani, an indigenous people in what is today Paraguay, believed it was violating the animal's spirits to kill or hunt them before ceremonies were done. The Cherokee would practice ceremonial fasting and abstinence from sex to honor animals before the hunt.

Every indigenous tribe had ceremonies associated with their connection to the land. These added gratitude to their daily lives, especially to the animals and plants that sustained them. This is the experience I seek to create in myself and for others.

During Sacred Hunting experiences, we have at least one ceremony each day. We open the gathering together in ceremony, acknowledging the four directions, sharing tobacco as an offering, and verbally sharing our intentions for the experience. We have a closing ceremony that allows us to give thanks, share commitments, and embrace our brothers.

The centerpiece of the experience is a ceremony with power plants, accompanied by noble silence for introspection. In this time, fully immersed in nature and surrounded by the death that hunting brings, men have profound experiences.

I found Will crying profusely as he finally processed the suicide of a friend many years prior. I held Bryan as he sobbed reflecting on the death of his daughter, who he said had visited us in spirit as a bird. David felt guilt and shame as he remembered wounding an animal only a few hours prior to the ceremony.

The ceremonial experiences men have are far-ranging. Mike found resonance with a tree, which embodied to him all the virtues he aspired to. Jared experienced and fully expressed deep gratitude, joy, and laughter.

When I first started creating ceremony in my life and Sacred Hunting experiences, I felt like an imposter. I have experience with ceremonies from my Native American mentor, but I was not raised with anything resembling one and haven't been educated in any official lineage around ceremonies with plants.

It was challenging for me to create ceremony, as it felt contrived at first. In a world bereft of spiritual connection, I imagine this is a common feeling. We all yearn for a link with the divine, but few are taught how to achieve it.

The more positive experiences and reflections that men share with me, the more I have grown into accepting my capacity to hold ceremony for others. Ceremony, whether before or during the experience of hunting, is intentionality's culmination. It is what makes hunting sacred and is the wellspring from which these men and I find transformation.

EARTH AS RELATIVE

A good way to start thinking about nature, talk about it. Rather talk to it, talk to the rivers, to the lakes, to the winds as our relatives... the Earth, the rocks, the minerals, all of which you call "dead" are very much alive.
—John Lame Deer

BEFORE HUNTING, I HAVE EACH MAN CLOSE THEIR EYES, come into a grounded mental place, and imagine the animal they will hunt in their mind's eye. This process is one that brings a deeper connection to the animal, animating and personifying it. Most importantly, it changes the animal from a piece of flesh that provides us with meat, to a relative of sorts. In imagining that animal with its family, we cannot help but start to love it.

I want myself and the others who join my hunting experiences to acknowledge the kinship that many indigenous people had not only with animals, but with plants and rocks—*all* of Earth.

To the Shipibo of Peru, plants are teachers and wise elders. For the Lakota, the sweat lodge is filled with rock beings who heal those who enter. The aboriginal Australian people believe rocks are almost immortal, discovering the planet's wisdom in deep time.

In contrast, most westerners view plants as barely alive with little sentience. Plucking flowers, ripping off leaves, and breaking branches are commonplace, and the plant's experience is entirely disregarded.

It's easy to look at animals, especially mammals like cows and pigs, and see ourselves in them. They are the closest to our unique form of sentience, which we project to be "higher" thinking, a human-centric view of living things.

This view has spawned activist vegetarian and vegan groups. Many in these groups are good, empathetic people, but it is misguided to forget that all life and everything on this planet are sacred and alive.

The twenty-five-acre plot of land where I wrote much of this book is special because it was the first place I successfully hunted by myself. It was a place where I did plant and animal medicines, and which has consistently called me back. When a discussion with my spiritual teacher turned to my relationship to this acreage, he said that the land speaks to itself. Like a landlord asking for references, this terrain will ask others how I treat the Earth.

How would we treat natural places if we truly *felt* the world and all things in it were relatives? Not just a distant relative we have nothing in common with, but a grandmother who takes care of all of our needs and loves us more than even our own parents?

This belief brings me into a different relationship with hunting. I ask permission from the land to be there and acknowledge the predator relatives I share space with. I offer something or make a sacrifice in exchange for taking something from the land.

One rare, icy cold weekend in central Texas, I led a group of men on a medicine hike through hill country, moving through juniper, oak, and shrubland. Stopping for a rest, I experienced a connection to the plants, the rocks, and animals in our vicinity. I felt empathy for the ice-covered prickly pear cactus and juniper leaves, ill-equipped to handle freezing temperatures. I felt awe seeing the vibrant colors of limestone erupting from the earth.

Broadening our view of sentience and consciousness, we see the rocks, plants, water, and animals differently. We may even see them in a way that allows us to love them more.

MENTORSHIP

WALKING AMONG THE STARS

Our chief want in life is somebody who wil make us do what we can.
—Ralph Waldo Emerson

I FOLLOW WILL TAEGEL TOWARDS A JUNIPER TREE AT THE side of the road. The purple-blue berries are ripe and beckoning. Will goes silent for a moment, holding his hand up to the tree. It's obvious he is in some form of prayer or communication with the plant-being in front of us.

After his moment with the tree, Will checks if any berries are ready to come off the branch. He is careful to "ask for an offering," meaning that he applies light pressure to the berry, attuning to whether it is loose and ready to go, or firmer and unripe. From what I know of Will after seven years of mentorship, this is a quite ordinary way of communicating with and relating to the plants all around us and learning Earth's subtle teachings.

Will Taegel, also known as "Star Heart," his spirit name, is an elder and guide who straddles the connection of indigenous cultures and philosophies with western scientific and psychological research.

Will was trained in shamanic lineages of many cultures, including the Muskogee (Creek) and Lakota traditions and has been adopted by the Mexica Aztecs, among other indigenous peoples. His doctorates focus on ecopsychology and field physics, and he spent decades as a psychotherapist. He's an ordained Methodist minister who spent time in Martin Luther King Jr.'s congregation. I'm still amazed by the philosophers, researchers, and scholars whom he considers close personal friends.

Will exudes wisdom, humility, and many other virtues a young male like me gravitates toward—especially after being arrested and starting to reflect on existential questions. At the age of twenty-three, I either searched online or learned by word-of-mouth about the traditional sweat lodge ceremonies that he facilitated once a month on his land near Wimberley, Texas. They were part of the Earthtribe initiative that he created many years ago with his mentor, Bear Heart Williams, to return humans to Earth-based consciousness.

For reasons I couldn't then explain, I was drawn to Will "Star Heart" and the Earthtribe when I was often one of the youngest people, by three or four decades, to participate in the sweats. I skipped traditional Friday-night partying in my University of Texas dorm room to wake up early Saturday, drive forty-five minutes, and go through five hours of ceremony and ritual I didn't fully understand with considerably older people.

At the inexperienced, immature age when I first got to know him, I spoke with Will but didn't have the capacity to take in the wisdom he shared. He'd say things that made no real sense at the time but instinctively felt true and wise. Fortunately, I continued to listen to the message and the forces that brought me back to visit with Will.

As in many indigenous traditions, including the one Will and his mentor, Bear Heart Williams are part of, a council with an elder takes place while walking. I will often record Will as we walk, trying desperately to preserve all the wisdom my mind couldn't hold by itself. I sometimes bring questions, which he will respond to by email between our councils.

While on our walks, we stop and face every vehicle that drives by, waving to ensure we are safe. At times, we stop to connect with a plant or a tree, like the juniper that gives us a single berry to taste. We don't swallow the berry but put it in our mouths and chew it for a bit, tasting the rich cedar flavor.

This simple act reflects the bridge between eco-spirituality and science that Will walks. We pray, sing songs to, and establish a relationship with the tree. At the same time, we familiarize ourselves biologically with the juniper plant, so our bodies don't develop "cedar fever," an allergic reaction to airborne cedar pollen that can debilitate folks in central Texas for months.

Will leads by guiding, providing perspectives, concepts, and, most importantly, stories. He's helped me learn the subtle teachings of nature's plants and animals, distinct from the big visions that accompany entheogens like peyote or ayahuasca.

In my apprenticeship with Will, I have never felt wrong. He helped develop a psychological approach called inner council theory, where we look at our psyche not as a single self, but a council of sub-selves all vying for their needs, wants, and desires.

Sometimes my inner child wants one thing, and my warrior self wants another. We all experience dissonance in ourselves, and this provides a supportive, less judgmental way of viewing our psyches—less judgmental towards one another, less judgmental of my own actions, and less judgmental towards the men whom I now mentor.

Being mentored has integrated the hunting and ayahuasca experiences that sent me down my present path. In retrospect, I can clearly see the sequence of events that led me to the work I am doing, including writing this book.

When they happened, I was unsure. One of the first things Will told me when I returned from my ayahuasca journeys was, "The plants chose you." He meant the plants are sentient and want me to speak a message the Earth needs on their behalf.

Will would later say that the Earth was calling me to help her. Another phrase he used was, "Earth is saving herself through you." For someone who had just developed a relationship with higher power, this felt true. Free from any religious upbringing, I was a blank slate and received the belief that the Earth is that higher power with open arms.

Reflecting on my journey, I can say definitively that I would not be where I am without Will Taegel's mentorship. He has guided me to the wisdom of my prison experience, without judgment and with forgiveness. He has supported me through the loss of an intimate partner, and most importantly, he has helped shape my worldview, the relationship I have with Earth, higher power, my dharma, and the community of men whom I am building around me to pass down his teachings.

QUANAH PARKER

The hunter must not only know about the habits of his prey, he also must know that there are powers on this earth that guide men and animals and everything that is living.
—CARLOS CASTANEDA

IN AN EMPIRE THAT SPANNED HUNDREDS OF THOUSANDS of square miles and encompassed the modern states of Texas, New Mexico, Colorado, Oklahoma, and Kansas, as well as northern Mexico, the Comanche considered the canyonlands of the Texas Panhandle to be among their holiest spiritual sites. In Palo Duro and Caprock Canyons, Comanche chiefs like the famed Quanah Parker would fast and vision quest for guidance for themselves and their people.

Quanah Parker was the last chief of the Comanche tribe before they were forced on the reservation. He was half-Comanche and half-white—his mother, Cynthia Ann Parker, had been kidnapped as a child, raised as Comanche, and married a chief.

Quanah was a ferocious warrior and Comanche leader when the tribe was at war with the U.S. military. But on the reservation, when the wars were over, he also found a place as a peaceful chieftain and rancher.

Unlike many North American chiefs who could not assimilate into western life, Quanah adapted so well that he even became great friends with Theodore Roosevelt, then president of the United States. Quanah was a "bridgewalker," a term Will "Star Heart" uses for those who are bridges between opposing cultures or worldviews. He is a role model and spirit guide I feel deeply connected to, and for whom I have great respect.

Towards the end of the bitter Comanche war that had raged for thirty years, Parker sought guidance as his people struggled to maintain their culture and way of life. As the legend goes, Quanah Parker visited the top of a mesa to meditate and prayed to the Great Spirit for guidance or a sign that would inform the direction he would take for his people.

Two things then happened. First, he saw a wolf that howled at him and then ran in the direction of nearby Fort Sill. Second, he saw an eagle who swooped down at him before flying northeast toward the same fort. For Quanah, this was guidance that he needed to surrender his band of Quahadi Comanche there.

Quanah Parker and the Comanche treated nature as a guide, as do all indigenous people intimately connected with the Earth's nuances.

Ringing the Caprock and Palo Duro Canyons is a special type of sage called *ke-war-re-nu* or "sand sage" in English. The Comanche considered this sage sacred and rubbed it on their skin as a form of bathing. I often use it before hunting trips that I facilitate.

One summer, Will "Star Heart" asked me to collect some *ke-war-re-nu* for him. The day was warm, like most July days in Texas. Parking my vehicle and crossing an infrequently traversed highway, I found several patches of *ke-war-re-nu*. Speaking to it, saying prayers, and intentionally taking small portions from many different trees, I heard a snap and crack. An old tree fell by the riverbank. Looking around, I realized there were no other humans nearby. The tree, most likely over one or two hundred years old, had fallen by itself at precisely the moment I was there. The experience was a new one that felt auspicious.

On the next long day of driving, I saw six hawks of various kinds, another sign that I couldn't then decipher. For many indigenous North American cultures, the hawk indicates a higher perspective or greater vision. The "winged beings" soar high above the earth, seeing things with more depth and clarity.

Having seen these two signs, I remembered an old practice Will taught me. Between 2 and 4 a.m., the veil between the dream world and waking reality is thinner. In this liminal space, one can ask questions of the other world. This isn't always an easy endeavor, and oftentimes, in my dream state, I just forget to ask.

But this night was different. As I was dreaming about driving a car, a giant vulture slammed into my windshield, startling me "awake." As I gasped for air, this vulture messenger reminded me to speak to the "winged beings."

"Winged beings, what does this mean?"

"Go ahead!"

"Winged beings, what are you trying to teach me?"

"Fulfill your destiny."

"What is my destiny?"

"Hunting!"

The teachings felt intuitively true. In relating the encounter to Will, he reminded me that I had picked the sage from Los Lingos Creek, which means "tongue" in English, a meaningful sign to him that Earth was speaking to me using the mother tongue.

Over the course of that trip, I would go on to find golden feathers, see a great horned owl, and witness a screeching golden eagle.

The meaning I ascribed to these events was my own. Like Quanah Parker, I conceptualized and interpreted my experiences with humility in the best way I could. I understood my attunement to and refinement of Earth's teachings were still in their infancy.

What attunement I have since developed has been catalyzed by my hunting practice. The more deeply I cultivate the practice of hunting, the more deeply I empathize and become one with those teachings.

John Vaillant wrote, "Successful hunting is an act of terminal empathy. The kill depends on how successfully the hunter inserts himself into the mind of his prey." Once I can insert myself in the mind of my prey, I can insert myself into the mind of other creatures and, more importantly, into the eco-field.

This eco-field is what Will calls a "more-than-human language," a connection point between humans and their surrounding environment.

We're all guided by some force in our lives. If we're lucky, we're stimulated to grow into more self-actualized and self-expressive individuals. Where that stimulation comes from varies. Often, our interests or growth come from the reflections of other individuals or society more broadly. An overweight person may prioritize losing weight after hearing an insensitive comment.

Allowing nature to be my guide, I have the opportunity to explore what is true, intuitive, and alive for me. My natural environment leads the way, and this is what Quanah Parker would have done.

I have such an affinity with and connection to Quanah Parker, his framed portrait hangs in my office. One day, Paul Chek stopped our conversation mid-sentence and said,

> *He knows who you are. There is a ray of energy coming from that image directly into your heart chakra. He's listening to you right now and he's with you right now...That being there is interested in you.*

Had that come from anyone besides Paul Chek, a well-respected holistic health teacher and wise elder with documented clairvoyant capabilities, I would not have taken it seriously. Coming from him, I was awestruck by the connection to my highest role model.

Chek advised me to connect with Parker from a spiritual perspective and receive whatever message I was meant to receive. The next morning, I went into a medicine ceremony with the intention of opening my heart chakra and listening to Quanah Parker's spirit. In ceremony, I saw him put his hand on my shoulder and say, "I am you and you are me."

Will "Star Heart" again helped me integrate the experience, recognizing that the same Earth, plants, trees, and animals that birthed Quanah Parker also birthed Will and me. We are all from this land of Texas.

The same Earth consciousness that birthed my Sacred Hunting endeavor also birthed a crucial event in Parker's life. While he was living on the reservation, Teddy Roosevelt visited Oklahoma with an entourage of Anglo-American politicians and businessmen. Parker took these men on a hunt where he introduced them to Comanche rites and rituals. In my mind, this was the first sacred hunt conducted with the same intention I have adopted in my work.

Quanah Parker, a half-breed bridgewalker, facilitated a spiritual and sacred way of hunting to a group of influential people, sharing a new form of consciousness. If I can embody half the virtues of this man, the world will be the better for it.

SACRED FEMININE

> *The feminine always seems chaotic and complicated from the perspective of the masculine...the feminine energy itself is undirected but immense, like the wind and deep currents of the ocean, ever changing, beautiful, destructive, and the source of life.*
> —David Deida

RAW LAND IN CENTRAL TEXAS, RARELY MAINTAINED OR manicured, can be a thick tangle of shrubby cedar, prickly agarita, with hints of prairie grass which indicate a landscape of the past quite different from today's. In the wilds of this overrun landscape are creatures who have adapted to the thorns, the brush, and secrecy.

When I first arrived on twenty-five acres of unmanaged hill country seventy miles west of Austin, the land was overgrown, and the stories it told were hard to decipher. It was the first private land I'd been given permission to hunt on, a luxury in the mostly privately owned state of Texas. On that raw land, it was my responsibility to find game that I could hunt, and I was in charge of reading an unfamiliar landscape.

The first clue was the game trails. Animals will walk habitually in the same pattern to develop trails, so they can expend less energy moving through brush. If they took a different route each time, they would expend far more energy in a world where the margins of survival are thin. On this land, the relative openness of game trails was in stark contrast to the thickly wooded surroundings.

The more trails I followed, the more intersections I reached. Some were dead ends leading me into brush that reminded me, with a humbling scratch or poke, who was really in charge. But patience took me into what seemed like a highway of crisscrossing trails much trafficked by all manner of animals.

This was my spot. Though it's often best to set an ambush around water or food, I had limited space and an intuition that the highway of trails would bring an animal to that vicinity. I set up, with a small tent enclosure to block my scent, and sat, waited, and watched.

My hypothesis was correct, but that didn't mean success. Animals would come through, but quickly, en route to somewhere else. Rarely did they stop long enough for me to take a shot, and my frustration grew.

The remnants of late summer started to fade over the weeks. When autumn came, the acorns fell. Suddenly, deer were spending more time near where I was hiding. Male deer noticed the subtle changes in the environment more thoroughly than I did. They started showing themselves, chasing females at times, as mating season had begun.

Like sensory organs, my body and brain filtered everything I noticed. I was witnessing the environment, recognizing patterns, and making decisions based upon a deepening subtle knowledge.

The Earth was training me to attune to her feminine essence. When I witness nature while hunting, I'm in tune with my natural surroundings differently than if I were camping or hiking. I'm in quiet contemplation, allowing the surrounding landscape to teach me what is true and real in that moment—that day, that week, and that season in time, for that precise location.

Attunement to the landscape we live in used to be a birthright necessary for our species' survival, and that landscape made its way into our myths, traditions, and ceremonies. The alienation from the environment we now feel is like the lack of clarity about our inner emotional landscapes.

These inner emotional and psychological landscapes are foreign to many, especially men. Just as most people walk through the forest blind to the clues surrounding them, they are blind to the wisdom held in their bodies:

their intuition, and the emotions and feelings that unconsciously guide their every action. I was blind to them for much of my life.

If only we have the vision and knowledge to comprehend the landscape, there are always lessons to learn. This often requires stillness, patience, and practice, whether one is navigating the physical landscape to hunt for deer, or the inner landscape to come to terms with a divorce or death of a loved one.

Attuning to our inner landscape means recognizing and integrating all the parts of ourselves. We all have an inner child, a boy or girl who needs to be heard even when we make adult decisions. We all have a wild man or woman; we have our ego and our heart. We have a rich array of inner voices that sit in our inner council. Just as attunement to the forest takes much time, so does deeper awareness of the inner workings of our mind and psyche.

Until I was twenty-five years old, I had no knowledge of or connection to the wild landscape surrounding me. I was similarly disconnected from my emotions and feelings. This division led me to unconscious and immoral behaviors, for which I paid the price in prison.

Today, it feels special to walk in central Texas, to know my physical surroundings and how those surroundings lead me to the animals I hunt. I feel at home in the woods now, as I do in my own feelings. My inner council attunes to every situation in my life.

Attunement to the inner feminine within myself is a step towards greater connection to the women in my life. How a man relates to the Earth is how he relates to a woman.

In our current collective consciousness, the basic, unconscious way men see Earth and women is in terms of what they can extract or gain. In the case of Earth, this mentality is the source of strip mines, water pollution, and factory farms. In the case of women, it is usually dedicated to sex or attention.

When I relate with a new lover, I don't immediately know her preferences, desires, or boundaries. I learn from her in deepening intimacy and attune to her body, her movements, her expressions, her words. I also deepen my intimacy with the feminine as I learn animal behaviors, seasonal changes, and which plants are edible and medicinal.

Relating with Earth, as with a woman, is not only about love and intimacy. The feminine in either a woman or Earth will test me to feel my strength—and weak spots.

Sometimes I fail her tests, and this will cause me grief and sadness. I remember a particular elk-hunting experience in the Sawtooth Mountains of Idaho. After a fifty-mile week of climbing mountains, my sole shot penetrated four inches to the left and ended in failure. Tears were shed, and it took me nearly three weeks to recover emotionally.

To be strong as a man is to give love even when I feel hurt. David Deida, the great teacher of masculinity, reminds me to heal my wounds and return to loving fully. The more I do, the more the feminine opens, and the more the masculine receives her gifts. I've never loved or been nurtured and supported by the feminine as I am today through the Earth.

If I open my heart to learning from the feminine, I will treat her with humility and respect, and create a sacred union. Just as an emotionally connected relationship with a woman is more fulfilling than sex alone, so is having a relationship with Earth that transcends what resources I can extract.

Every man yearns for a relationship with the feminine. Society often teaches us that it must be solely in the form of romantic connection with women. But we can connect with the sacred feminine within us and the natural world surrounding us and bring that foundation into our intimate partnerships.

PURSUIT

WHERE THE PATH LEADS

Transformation in life is like tracking an animal. Find the first track and don't think too far ahead.
—Boyd Varty

A MOVING DEER CREATES A DISTINCT PATH ACROSS THE landscape. Blazing a path is hard work, taking resources and energy often in short supply for wild animals. Living on the razor's edge of life and death, animals conserve energy when they can. They habituate to the same trails, which become well-trafficked highways.

Hunters recognize this path as a "game trail," while others barely recognize it at all.

Once you see the game trails, they become psychoactive. You can't unsee them. They are another word, phrase, or syllable in Earth's language. They also beckon you to follow. Like a mythical story or folklore, the path leads into the unknown.

Our lives are comparable. It's hard at first to recognize the paths among the landscape. Conditioning from our parents, the media, and our civilization creates noise and confusion, and with no connection to life-navigation skills, we even forget what the path looks like.

Rarely does a game trail lead me, bow in hand, to prey. I follow it anyway. More often than not, it leads me through terrain I may never have visited. I see new species and I find deer signs or something else unexpected.

More importantly, I feel excitement when I follow a game trail. It's an enlivening clue that leads to potential prey. Finding and following a trail is like finding my "dharma," calling, or life's path. I don't know where I'm going to end up, but I feel alive.

It turns out that following such trails is the easiest way to move through most terrain. A thorny thwacking is a common occurrence while hunting in the backcountry. It's not fun and is hard on the body.

Eschewing the path parents or society desire for you, following your unique path, is both harder and easier. Easier because you can live with fewer regrets, knowing that you took that path.

ACTIVE PATIENCE

BACK HUNCHED, HANDS DEEP IN MY POCKETS, I SEE THE first rays of sunlight penetrate the dark night. The ambient temperature is coldest in the moments before dawn. These rays provide hope, a sign that the world is coming alive, and I can do my work soon.

Animals move as silhouettes in the darkness, unseen and unknown. Some may be the deer I'm hunting; others are smaller critters finding their bearings.

Sitting in a deer blind or tree stand is a test of patience and endurance. When the body doesn't move, the cold becomes withering. The hours of waiting patiently but actively take a mental toll, especially when they begin at 5:00 a.m.

The sun's rays peak over outcroppings, and warmth slowly invites my hands out from inside my pockets onto my smooth, cold bow. The landscape comes alive faster than you would imagine due to physics and the Earth's curvature. Birds sing, bugs buzz, and diurnal animals begin to move.

Once I can see clearly, my attention is focused on my surroundings. This is an active patience. I may wait for hours upon hours, but the whole time my mind should be taking in the landscape and analyzing every movement, something I wish I could do more often.

With enough time, a hunter becomes finely tuned to the environment. Primary perception soaks in raw data, colors, and shapes, while resisting the urge to classify anything as irrelevant. Secondary perception then filters, processes, and labels the environment, removing distractions to focus on what's compelling.

The movement of vertical stacks of grass doesn't catch my eye, but the slightest horizontal shift is analyzed and interpreted. The long line of a deer's back sticks out in the landscape.

On this particular morning, I may see a few animals in four hours of hunting, or I may see none. That is part of the hunt.

On a group hunt I facilitated, three men and I had been hunting for hours, moving slowly across the landscape. We found some deer and elk, but none belonged to species we could hunt that time of year.

I later took a moment away from the group atop a high point, peering through my binoculars at a distant ridge. Seeing a herd of animals we could hunt, the first of the morning, I immediately walked down and told them to follow me. One man would later recount that my entire demeanor had changed. I went from leading a leisurely stroll through beautiful landscape to having a sense of urgency, a mission, and a purpose. A hunter often seems complacent or bored until the moment of truth arrives.

Active patience is the capacity to wait long periods with readiness and poise for the rare opportunity. As a hunter, I may choose to succumb to the boredom, which sometimes humbles me. Cell service is ubiquitous, and I can fall victim to responding to texts. Such complacency has lost me many opportunities. At other times, I'm moving too quickly, processing my environment as irrelevant, when it isn't.

How much of our lives is waiting patiently with readiness for the few moments of opportunity? If we succumb to complacency or boredom, we can easily slide into vices that don't serve us like checking my phone when my attention should be on the surroundings. Binge eating, watching Netflix, pornography, and alcohol come into our lives, dulling our capacities for the moments we need them most.

Our mission or purpose on Earth requires these capacities. My mission on the hunt is to find an animal to kill, but we all have a greater mission in our lives. In traditional Hindu texts, this is called "dharma" or "life's path." For some people it is parenting, for others it's meaningful relationships or a vocation.

In day-to-day existence, our routine responsibilities may feel disconnected from our mission, but this is precisely where active patience is critical.

Maintaining active patience, on the hunt or in our lives, is not only valuable as a means of achieving what we desire. The stillness thrust upon us as we wait patiently can be one of the most contemplative states we experience.

When I am engrossed in my surroundings, I recognize the odd shapes of rocks, see the native baby bluestem grass swaying gently in the wind, and acknowledge the healthy soil. A bird tweets and flies off, chased by another in a playful or courtship ritual.

There is a stillness that comes from hunting that cannot be replicated while camping or bird-watching. The stakes are higher, the intent bigger, and life or death is on the line. The stillness that accompanies such a perspective is one that is deeply embedded in the fiber of our being, because our species has hunted for so long.

This stillness, which is the foundation of contemplative practice, contrasts starkly to our civilized world. Technology giants like Google and Facebook employ psychologists to help capture our attention and engagement. Short video clips reduce our concentration, and distractions abound. When I'm trapped in my phone's vortex, it's easy to feel scatterbrained, like a ping-pong ball is being smacked against the inner walls of my skull.

Hunting with active patience creates a stillness that heals all this. I'm in my environment and present with nature in a way that I can't be otherwise. I'm engaged with a mission and purpose, attentive to the changes and movements in the landscape. My entire body and mind become a giant sensory organ, scanning the landscape, seeing the whole picture and variations in patterns, then focusing on the detail. My eyes see, my ears listen to leaves crackle and birds sing, and my body feels the wind.

This is a skill I must cultivate to be successful on the hunt and in my life, one I've had the privilege of learning.

LONELINESS

The capacity to be alone is the capacity to love.
—Osho

SITTING ATOP A RIDGE IN THE SAWTOOTH MOUNTAINS OF Idaho, I turned to my hunting guide and shared the loneliness I felt in that moment. With my documentary film crew back at camp, the last light of day slipping beneath the horizon, and nothing but mountains and trees for miles, I felt a deep sense of distance and seclusion that was both debilitating and enriching.

My guide acknowledged the feeling, recognizing the accompanying tranquility, as we continued to sit in silence.

Whether I'm hunting on public land far from civilization or sitting in a deer blind near my house, I'm forced into presence and attentiveness. There's nothing to distract me from the reality that I am alone. I must be present to all of the sensations, feelings, emotions, and thoughts that come into my mind, no matter how nerve-racking they may be. The hunt forces me to become intimate and comfortable with loneliness.

The loneliness I experience has roots in my childhood. My father's physical presence, contrasted with an absence of emotional depth and masculine mentoring, created feelings of loneliness when I was a boy.

Being closely enmeshed with my mother during tumultuous times created a bond that, when absent, came with its own flavor of loneliness. Add to my personal story the explosion of loneliness that disintegrating nuclear families and isolated individuals experience throughout America. All of us need healing work.

I've realized that loneliness has less to do with those we're surrounded by than with our own experience of the world. I can be with other people and still feel lonely. Numbing mechanisms often dampen the willingness to process feelings and traumas.

Stimulants like caffeine and amphetamines allow us to achieve a "success" quantified by paychecks and bank accounts. But they silence the voice inside that desires meaning. Alcohol and drug abuse is rampant. Cell phones and social media provide us a feeling of being with friends and people, but without the nourishment that deep connection provides.

Hunting in the vast wilderness has become my loneliness therapy. I have a romantic view of the wild, and from the comfort of my home, connected to friends and my phone, I look forward to my next journey.

But when I'm hunting, I feel resistance. I can sense the part of myself that desires to leave the woods so I can also leave the harsh inner critic behind, a sub-self we all have in our lives. Instead of listening to the resistance, I lean into the discomfort, allow the woods to bring up the emotions and feelings associated with loneliness, work with them, heal, and grow.

MITAKUYE OYASIN: ALL ARE RELATED

PERMISSION

When we killed a buffalo, we knew what we were doing. We apologized to his spirit, tried to make him understand why we did it, honoring with a prayer the bones of those who gave their flesh to keep us alive, brothers, the buffalo nation, as well as for our own people.
—John Lame Deer

I see a female deer with her neck bent low, eating a fig from the ground. A fig tree stands to her right, and I am on her left, looking into the distance, with my left hand on her gray hide. This was my vision, an answer to the question: "What is the next evolution in my service to Earth?" I participated in an ayahuasca ceremony where this vision and changed perspective on my relationship with land emerged.

The absurdity of the idea that I could "own" land became present for me. In my and most indigenous peoples' belief systems, the land is the Goddess. We humans cannot own our higher power. Even the word "steward" didn't resonate, as it supposes that the wisdom of the Earth is not enough, that humans know what's best for Her. What did resonate was "partnership."

Ayahuasca creates feelings of extreme empathy, and I was able to vividly imagine what it would be like to have a partner relationship to land. I would grow a fruit forest that the birds, bees, and bugs could share. I would offer eggs to the snakes and find ways to preserve and nurture the coyote and wild hogs that are so commonly killed on sight.

This vision depicts Earth and land as a deity or force larger than ourselves, worthy of our reverence and service. It humbly acknowledges that Earth provides the resources for all humans to survive and thrive and recognizes the immense power and destructive capacity she wields.

This perspective causes me to ask permission to go out on the land before every hunt.

When I arrive, either alone or with the groups I facilitate, I have a moment with the land as I spread tobacco as an offering and say a prayer. North American tribes believed tobacco to be one of the most sacred plants. It was so valuable that it was used as a store of value and exchange, like money. By giving tobacco to the Earth, I am paying my respect and the dues I owe the land for the opportunity to hunt and feed myself.

There are times when I must listen to the intuition that the land does not want me to hunt at that time. There are situations where I have received the message that a particular weekend was not a good time, and I must respect that boundary, whatever its source.

In indigenous cultures, it is common to believe that some animals sacrifice themselves to hunters if we humans agree to protect the rest. If we have a relationship to the land where we are serving the greater whole, we may sustain ourselves with the individual animals that we kill.

This has often felt true. Mike Pullano hunted for the first time on a group hunt using a rifle that he had only fired a few times. Within a couple hours of going out near sunset, he had an opportunity and shot and killed a deer. It was a profound and rewarding experience for him.

Over a month later, while recounting the story of his hunt with a friend, he realized that the animal had given her life for him as a sacrifice. He recognized that he was unskilled at that time, didn't know what he was doing, and the miraculously perfect success he had was an offering from the Earth.

When I have felt in harmony with the land, treated her with respect, and asked permission, many examples of this have occurred.

Another word for permission, one that has become increasingly important in a world seeking greater equality, is consent. The extractive, entitled, and abusive way modern western civilization treats land reflects how men have often treated women. The reason sexual violence and transgressions are perpetrated so frequently is not necessarily because men are bad, but because they have numbed themselves to women's signals and boundaries.

Men can have tunnel vision when seeking to extract what they desire, such as sex. I don't believe men need to ask permission for every step of intimacy, but they need to attune to a woman's body as we learn to attune to Earth's rhythms. Both are boundaries in their own way.

The way that I treat one thing in my life is the way I treat everything. If I treat the land as an object to be taken from, extracted, and beaten into submission despite her complaints, I am hurting myself as well as the land. I must have the respect and reverence to ask permission for every animal and plant that I take from the land.

COHERENCE

The wild does not value hierarchy. Only presence.
—Boyd Varty

THE WIND BEGAN TO HOWL MORE BITTERLY AS MY HOSTS and I crested a snow-capped ridge in the Bighorn Mountains. Even from the comfort of our warm truck, it was clear we were entering a new climatic zone. I later learned from the Crow Indians that this was called "Windy Point," an aptly named, towering region of the Bighorn Mountains, with centuries of myth and history.

After putting several layers of clothing on, I slipped outside to look into the valley with my binoculars. Despite the howling wind and deep snow on the ground, the sun was shining brightly at the top of the mountain, and its warmth made being outside bearable. I peered through the binoculars at brown specks on the horizon: bison. One of the last remaining free-ranging bison herds in the world inhabits the lower valleys of the Bighorn Mountains on the Crow reservation in eastern Montana.

From this expansive place, within the context of the indigenous people who have lived there for millennia, it felt like I was looking back in time. The Crow, Lakota, and earlier tribes, going back tens of thousands of years, were peering into that valley looking for the same animals with the same motivations and aims.

When I think like our ancestors, looking for the same food and employing the same tactics in the same territory, I have created a portal where I can meld my mind and psyche with those people. What I'm doing in that moment aligns with what these people have done for thousands of years. I can use this link to learn ways of being other than hunting.

These peoples were more egalitarian, freer, more collaborative, and better connected with the web of ecology all around them. As I establish a bond with them while hunting, I also find glimpses of their worldview that I can bring back into my "civilized" twenty-first-century life.

One unmistakable example is the openness to sharing meat that is part of my hunting practice. Generally speaking, meat is the most expensive food, especially when high quality and ethically sourced. When I used to buy meat from the grocery store, I had no desire to share it with anyone. It was expensive, I had bought it with my own money, and it was mine. An understandable, if selfish, attitude.

When I've hunted meat, it costs much more in both time and money. But I want to share it with others. It feels like an imperative to feed the people who are in my tribe with meat that I have killed—to share the stories and create kinship.

This is what our ancestors would have done. One person's kill was food to be shared with everyone. The whole tribe was in it together, as a collective unit of mutual support.

When a Kung bushman living in West Africa was asked where the best place was to store excess meat from a hunt, he quipped that it was in his friend's belly. If he shared his kill with all his friends, the reciprocity when the others were successful would keep him full and content.

In the Navajo tradition, the tribe celebrates the group of men who have gone out to kill an animal, not the individual. They honor the band who participates in bringing the bounty back to the tribe.

The stronger the bonds I have with the people who walked the Earth before me, the better man I become. I'm more connected to the Earth, less selfish, more collaborative, more open and supportive. Hunting is an embodied activity that allows me to *feel* the way our ancestors felt. That feels so much like home that I have no desire to go back.

PREDATORS

MID-AFTERNOON ON A WARM, HUMID TEXAS DAY, MY teacher, Will "Star Heart," and his wife, Judith, came face to face with a Timber rattlesnake. A camper ran to Will, who was finishing dinner, exclaiming that a snake was near his tent.

Will's teacher, Bear Heart Williams, immediately came to mind. Three decades earlier, Bear Heart, a full-blooded Muskogee native American medicine man, had shared with him the meaningful relationship that many indigenous people have with predators and the snake in particular.

"In my tribe, we were always told that snakes are our little brothers. We should never be afraid of them. Respect them? Yes. Know their danger? Yes. But we learned that if you let your fears run you, your negativity will attract their attention. The proper thing to do is to honor them."

For Bear Heart and many indigenous people, singing songs is one way to connect with creatures with whom we share no verbal language. It's as if even if the words aren't understood, the language of rhythm and energetics of the words put them at ease.

Will remembered that teaching when faced with a rattlesnake that hot, humid, Texas afternoon. Humming medicine songs to himself, he found a nearby shed, grabbed a rake, and found his way to the snake.

Those songs served him well. The snake quickly and painlessly offered her head onto and wrapped her body around the rake. As Will carried the snake five acres away to provide a wide berth, other campers approached with their culturally induced fears and anxieties. As if sensing the energy of these newcomers, the snake rattled next to Will's hands. Although this startled him, Will found a nice resting ground near a flowing creek with ample prey for his slithering friend.

Bear Heart has passed Will's worldview down to me. The respect, admiration, and cooperation I have as a hunter and outdoorsman sharing space with other apex predators has led me to practices that connect me with their spirits.

Connecting with the spirit of a clan, such as the snake clan, mountain lion clan, or bear clan, involves developing a relationship with the "oversoul" or representative of a family of animals. One example is my rescue of a Texas hognose snake. This species is not poisonous but utilizes what's called Batesian mimicry, after the English naturalist, Henry Walter Bates: an evolutionary survival mechanism whereby the snake looks like another, more poisonous relative—in this case the rattlesnake. In caretaking, holding, and singing to this snake, I ask her to warn her relatives in other realms that my band of hunters and I are coming.

The other apex predator in west Texas and the Texas Hill Country, where I frequently hunt, is the mountain lion. My two cats, traumatized as kittens by Hurricane Harvey, are distant relatives of the powerful, majestic, and often elusive mountain lion with whom I share space. The way one treats, respects, and honors the animals and plants in one's care is a direct reflection of one's perception of and relationship to Earth.

There are many ways of developing a relationship with predators. I support these animals, just as they support me on the hunt. I connect with them in medicine ceremonies and dreams.

Examples of this close relationship are found in indigenous cultures around the world. In the Siberian region of Primorsky Krai, a peninsula that faces the Pacific coast and Japan, the Nanai and Udege people have an intimate relationship with what is arguably the deadliest apex predator on the planet.

The Amur or Siberian tiger stands three feet tall and nine feet long, weighing 600 pounds, with claws as long and sharp as a velociraptor. If such a creature existed in what is today the United States, western ranchers and farmers would have surely exterminated it. Instead, the Nanai and Udege revere the Amur tiger, seeing it as an almost-mythic deity they share the land with.

Their culture requires them to give the tiger offerings. Sometimes this comes in the form of hunted meat. Sometimes it comes in the form of a trusted canine companion that does not make it through a snowy night. The people understand that a beloved dog, sometimes dying, is part of sharing space with the Amur tiger.

It's said if a man kills an Amur tiger, he himself will be killed. And if a tiger were to kill a human, its own kind would hunt that tiger down. There is a pact and a taboo between man and tiger.

In my experience, most westerners don't have this relationship with the predators with whom they share space. Hunters and ranchers often seek to exterminate coyotes, snakes, wolves, and mountain lions to protect their livelihood. While this is understandable, they are breaking the age-old compact we have with these other predators.

These people have experience with and a healthy respect for predators, but their fear compels them to kill. Often, urban dwellers with no experience or knowledge of the predator's true capabilities naively advocate on their behalf, not fully acknowledging their lethality. Both sides of the debate can learn from our indigenous ancestors.

As I shared my hunting experiences and my desire to bring them to other men and women, Will taught me an older, more connected way of being in relationship with predators. Will's teacher said, "Someday, you are going to be an elder...somebody is going to discover snakes close to humans. There will be several *someones* who want to kill the snake. They are not bad people. They are just acting out of what they have been taught. They think they are protecting the encampment but are really putting it in danger."

Our relationship with predators is a parable of our relationship with our environment as a whole. If we choose to see ourselves as separate from and needing to dominate the Earth, we will fear all that stands in the way of getting what we want. If we choose to see ourselves as a small part of a much larger web, we can more readily live in harmony both with other species and other humans.

STALKING

ONENESS

In the act of hunting, a man becomes, however briefly, part of nature again. He returns to the natural state, becomes one with the animal, and is freed of the existential split: to be part of nature and to transcend it by virtue of his consciousness.
—Erich Fromm

BINOCULARS IN HAND, I SLOWLY BENT MY TORSO TO MY left to whisper instructions to Stefanos, who had a female white-tailed deer in his sights. A world-class men's coach and facilitator, his childhood wounding had been alchemized into the healer and man who is my friend.

At the moment I was closest to him and his rifle, he fired at the animal. The shot rang in my ears. As I opened and shut my jaw to adjust to the sound, I tracked the deer with my binoculars. The shot had just missed over her back. She was unharmed and stood there momentarily confused. Before we had another opportunity, she left our sight.

We moved in close to verify there was no blood. I immediately moved into supporting Stefanos, who was frustrated at himself for having missed the shot.

"A clean miss is the second-best thing you could hope for," I told him. Wounding an animal feels way worse. "There is a lesson here intended for you specifically."

I fully trust the wisdom of each man's experience and help guide them to derive their own meaning from it.

I had an intuition that Stefanos would have another opportunity within a few minutes. These intuitions, or "spidey sense" as my hunting mentor, Marc, calls them, become more frequent and harder to ignore the longer you hunt.

Walking back to our camp, I could see Stefanos processing the experience, repeating it in his head. I walked the fine line between letting him alone with his experience and telling him he needed to keep his head up, because he was going to get another shot.

Within twenty minutes, we had again found deer unaware of our presence, perfect targets to pursue. Using the cover of a large, isolated oak tree, we snuck to within 150 yards of three white-tailed deer browsing for food. The largest came into position. Stefanos took control of his aim and shot the animal straight through the heart. The deer didn't even move. It went straight down where it was shot and died shortly thereafter.

The first instinct when you see an animal go down like that is to go over and see him. Sometimes, that's okay. In this instance, I wanted to give it some time and just be with the moment and the other two deer who had seen the death. They had not moved, and the other hunter with us could have had a shot, but I wanted us to simply witness the experience.

The deer walked straight to the dead animal, sniffed, and looked around. I took a knee realizing that we were witnessing this animal's family wondering where their loved one had gone. One moment, their brother, father, or cousin was alive. The next he was dead. Stefanos started to cry, as did I.

I cannot imagine the experience of watching a loved one unexpectedly dying before my eyes. In that moment, with empathy in our hearts, Stefanos and I had a glimpse into that reality. Regardless of the species, it's a powerful moment.

The undying awe, respect, and love for the animals I hunt come not *in spite* of the fact that I hunt deer, but *because* I hunt them.

Successful hunting requires deep empathy. To achieve a kill, I must insert myself into my prey's mind. I must know their needs and understand their fears and how the landscape alters their behavior. I must feel their thirst and hunger, not just comprehend it intellectually.

In this way, my heart opens to the animals I hunt in a special way. I feel love for the deer, elk, antelope, bear, bison, and every other animal I hunt.

This love is unique. It underpins my feeling of oneness not only with the animals, but also the plants that feed them, and the other animals that feed on them. The Lakota have a phrase for this, *mitakuye oyasin* meaning "we're all related." We are all connected. Hunting reminds me of this truth.

SURRENDER

PEERING THROUGH BINOCULARS AT THE TOP OF A RIDGE, I spotted the faint outline of a bull elk. Soon, the antlers appeared, and my excitement grew. At 500 yards, an expert sniper could have ended the hunt right then. But I was hunting with a compound bow and needed to get much closer.

A guide devised a plan based on the terrain in front of us. The elk was perched at the edge of a timber patch a couple of ravines in front of us. We would have to go back down the hill we were on, cross a stream and several ridges, and stay out of sight while moving as quickly as possible.

We spent nearly two hours traversing the short distance. Our approach was expertly positioned to account for the wind. At midday, the air currents would likely be moving up the ridge. Our job was to go far enough below the elk so he could not see or smell us, and then maneuver above him.

In almost all big-game hunting, the most important factor is the wind. Animals have evolved a sense of smell so refined it inspires awe. Because scent changes over time, it's as if an animal's sense of smell enables it to perceive the past. It's not a perception as we know it, but a much deeper, more instinctive understanding. Their prowess in picking up scent brings hunters into a deep, ever-present relationship with the wind.

At times, the wind is predictable. Hunting up a mountain in the morning is fairly foreseeable because thermal currents generally go downhill until later in the day. You're hunting into the wind or "have good wind," as hunters say.

But the wind can change rapidly, uncontrollably, and wreak havoc on plans. In certain topographies, wind can swirl around, changing directions frequently and without mercy, at least in the eyes of a frustrated hunter.

Because wind is one of the most important external factors influencing a hunt's success, it provides clues about the greater art of living. Despite our strategizing and intimate knowledge of hunting and the land, we're not in control.

The winds of life can change at any moment, for any reason. Maybe a loved one passes away, the planet succumbs to a pandemic, or finances become unstable. We cannot control every external event. Trying to do so is both futile and frustrating. The need to regulate our environment often comes from a place of fear. The capacity to surrender comes from a place of trust that everything will end up alright in the end.

This does not mean giving up or acquiescing. It simply means we must identify what's in our control and what isn't to better adapt to the situation.

An animal that catches my human scent becomes exponentially harder to hunt. If I dig my heels in, determined to hunt the animal no matter what, I'm likely doomed to fail. As opposed to moving on to another situation with better wind and dynamics. In the world of hunting, don't double down on failure. Surrender to what is out of control and move on to new opportunities.

The situation I found myself in while stalking the bull elk after two hours was tense and unenviable. Successfully reaching a ridge eighty yards above, my guide and I took off our shoes and started to gingerly stalk our prey. The closer one gets, the more challenging this becomes. We spent another hour getting to within forty yards of the elk.

Three hours into this venture, with feet hurting from stickers, thorns, and brush, I catch a glimpse of the elk lying down in midday tranquility. At that moment, yards away from a shooting opportunity, the wind changed, sending our human scent directly into the nostrils of the alert and attentive animal. After a quick turn of the head, he leapt to his feet and bounded away, foiling our entire afternoon.

In those challenging moments of our life when we have what we desire snatched away from us, it's common to ask why this happened. It may feel unjust and unfair. Sometimes it is.

But in surrender, we can gain something more powerful. We can get perspective and wisdom. The phrase "everything happens for us, not to us" is often repeated and has a lot of truth. Our perception of what happens to us changes how we respond. The wind changed on my stalk of the bull elk, because I was meant to be reminded of that life lesson.

We may feel grief or loss, and these are natural emotions to process. Surrender does not mean bypassing or suppressing emotions. I assuredly felt sadness and frustration after three hours of stalking that elk. But once the processing is complete, surrender beckons us to adapt and take the next steps.

THE SHOT

VOLITION

*Indigenous knowledge is not about the what,
it's about the how.*
—Tyson Yunkaporta

AS WAS CUSTOMARY IN INDIGENOUS CULTURES, A YOUNG boy aged twelve would be taught by his elders how to kill his first deer. To do this, the grandson was sent to his grandfather who, in his old age, spent time sitting in a rocking chair on his front porch.

"Grandfather, my parents say it's time for me to learn how to hunt to provide meat for my family, and you are to be my guide."

The grandfather nods quietly, ponders a moment, and replies, "I want you to go home and *imagine* seeing a deer before you go to bed at night."

After struggling with his imagination a couple of nights, the grandson finally completes the task. Eagerly returning to his grandfather, he receives the next instruction.

"I want you to go home and imagine seeing the deer and also that you are there with the deer."

The boy spent many nights, struggling to imagine the scenario his grandfather had laid out. By the time the grandson had successfully imagined himself with the deer, hunting season was over.

The grandson, young and impatient, became irate. "Grandfather, when am I going to learn how to hunt?"

"You're learning about hunting. The time will come for you to hunt."

When the next hunting season came around, the boy, now aged thirteen, was eager to begin. His first instruction of the season was: "Imagine you are there with the deer, but that the deer is coming towards you instead of you going towards the deer."

By this point, as any parent might guess, the grandson became even more impatient. "Grandpa, when do I get my gun? When do I start hunting?"

"Well, you're on your way, but you aren't there yet. I want you to go outside and sit under a tree. I want you to imagine the deer coming to you while you sit under the tree. Imagine the deer comes and you *commune* with the deer."

The boy starts to feel a developing connection. He completes this task, and grandfather instructs him to find the place in the forest that he saw in his imagination. This takes the rest of the season, but he succeeds in finding the spot he imagined.

He returns at age fourteen with a bit more patience, trusting the process unfolding in front of him. His grandfather then instructs him to sit in his spot in the forest, under a tree, and sing songs to the deer until the animal is drawn to him, just as he had imagined.

Day after day the deer showed up, coming closer to the grandson. Finally, the deer was next to him. In that moment of closeness and awe, the little boy opened his heart to the deer, and the deer opened his heart to him.

Upon hearing the heartfelt story, grandfather tells the boy, "Okay. It's time for you to find your bow or rifle and kill the deer now."

The process of connecting with the deer had so moved the boy that he balked at the idea. "No, I don't want to kill the deer. I'm friends with the deer now!"

But his grandfather insisted, "Your family needs the food. You have to hunt."

Begrudgingly, the boy returned to his spot. Caught between listening to his elder's instructions and the love he had developed for this animal, he worked himself into a rage, pounced on the deer, and cut its throat. Hauling the deer back to the porch, he threw it down and snorted, "There, old man! Are you satisfied?"

The grandfather sat in silence for a moment. He nodded in acknowledgment and took a deep breath. "When you can be as moved by stepping on a blade of grass as you are in killing this deer, then you'll be a man."

I share this parable with each man who attends a Sacred Hunting experience, because it portrays the intentionality and depth of feeling that accompanies or should accompany taking the life of another being. Taking the life of an animal or plant so that we may have sustenance to survive is a necessary fact of our existence. It's how we go about that killing that makes the difference.

Am I hunting solely for myself and my ego, filling the freezer with meat and mounting large antlers on my walls? That is one way to go about it.

Or am I hunting for myself, for the greater community I'll share the meat with, for the land and plants that need space to grow, for the deer to live on through me, and for the cosmos that beckons with this spiritual practice?

Indigenous wisdom reflects to me that what I do, such as killing an animal, is less important than how I do it.

My intention is not always pure. There are certainly times I succumb to my ego or desire to kill for myself or my business persona. I am human, after all.

But the ceremonies of smudging my weapons, cleansing them with herbs, such as sage and palo santo, and saying prayers to release all fear, anxiety, and hesitation remind me of the true expression of my higher self, so that my arrow may come from a place of genuine love for the animal and all connected to it.

Our lives are filled with crossroads, forks, and choices. We can project alternative universes in our imagination where the same choice comes from a place of fear or one of love. The same action, but with a different motivation, a different intention, and thus an entirely different energy and feeling.

There is often no right choice, only a choice made rightly. A world desensitized to volition may not recognize the difference.

On the hunt, I know when I'm coming from a place of love and when I'm not. This reality looks me in the face with beautiful eyes, large ears, and an inquisitive neck.

THE RIGHT SHOT

If there is a sacred moment in the ethical pursuit of game, it is the moment you release the arrow or touch off the fatal shot.
—Jim Posewitz

EVEN IN JANUARY, THE TEXAS HEAT CAN BE STIFLING. WHEN you're sitting in an insulated hunting blind, the heat becomes even more intense. Add the heavy-duty camouflage pants worn to survive walking through brush, and it feels like a sauna. Weather conditions are always a key element in the pursuit of wild game, but it makes the opportunity of a rewarding shot all the more intense and exciting.

A white-tailed doe, fat and skittish, walked into my vicinity. Either she had experienced many hunts before, or she was genetically predisposed to alertness. She was constantly looking around, sensing, probing, even running away when she thought something wasn't quite right. She was the most frightened-looking deer I've ever seen.

I had numerous opportunities to take a shot, but never the right one. Over the course of the weekend, she had literally or figuratively dodged four arrows. By the end, she had completely stumped me.

I had had shooting opportunities, but none were first-rate. A younger, white-tailed buck, who came into my shooting lane, was much easier to kill.

Then the doe "jumped the string," a term used to describe when an animal hears the "twang" of the arrow leaving the bow and reacts quickly enough to dodge it. I sent an arrow directly over her back. If an animal dodging an arrow moving faster than 300 feet per second doesn't inspire awe, respect, and wonder, I don't know what will.

After dodging one arrow, she came back into view, but was even more skittish. The dance was irritating, exciting, and nerve-racking at the same time.

Another young, white-tailed deer limped ten yards to my right, taking me by surprise. His left front hoof was broken and mangled. He limped heavily on his right foot, suffering, wilted, and seemingly diseased. He was so emaciated I could see his ribs. For a wounded animal, nature is unforgiving. Either the animal starves to death or meekly survives long enough to succumb to coyote or other predators.

I felt great empathy for this animal, and it overtook my rational, selfish desire to bring as much meat home from the hunting trip as I could. I felt conflicted at the time, but the truest and most energetic course of action was to use my arrow to take the life of this wounded deer and put it out of its misery. The right shot in this moment was a shot in service to the animal and a sacrifice of my personal desires.

The shot passed through the animal's heart, which was so bereft of blood that he was nearly impossible to track down. When we found the dead deer, we saw that it indeed had a disease or infection. I would receive no meat from this kill, which felt like a test from the universe.

Because I was hunting with a friend and sharing the meat, I apologized, rationalizing my actions. I had been caught between the egotistical world of killing meat for myself and the spirit world of killing an animal for Earth's sake. When a hunting mentor later told me that I had practiced proper ethics in the old traditions, I felt like I had passed a test.

For each shot taken on an animal is a physical, mental, emotional, and spiritual test. It is the point at which all of our morality, interpersonal work, courage, and shadow come to a head. My heart beats faster, adrenaline and dopamine flood my brain, and a concoction of other chemicals makes sure I vividly remember the moment in my mind's eye. A flow state is catalyzed. The rest of the world can fall away, and my process becomes the only thing that matters. I must regulate myself emotionally, acknowledging the death I'm bringing to the world, the life I'm ending, and the food I may be bringing home. I must be in spiritual alignment with myself, what I know to be right, and with my own form of higher power.

I've failed in all these areas at least once, sometimes more. Those failures have all been teaching and learning moments. Reminders to be humble and to honor and respect the animal and the practice of hunting above all else. The failures have helped me evolve to a place where I no longer want to take a shot at an animal. I want to take the right shot.

THE MISS

SHAME

> *If you put shame in a petri dish, it needs three ingredients to grow exponentially: secrecy, silence, and judgment. If you put the same amount of shame in the petri dish and douse it with empathy, it can't survive."*
> —Brené Brown

"Nock another arrow. Just shoot again," Marc said.

The elk was over fifty yards away, and I didn't have the pins sighted for that range. But after wounding the elk in the shoulder, I was told to shoot as many more arrows as possible while the elk still looked at me.

The second shot missed horribly. I was trying to process my first shot, realized I didn't have a way to aim, and felt the urgency behind Marc's instructions. It was the definition of a high-stress environment. As soon as the young bull elk realized something wasn't right and disappeared over the ridge, the botched job truly sank in.

So much had led me to that moment. I had been hunting elk over fifty miles in seven days, up and down mountains. I had traveled from Texas to Idaho. I had practiced extensively before the hunt and helped bring together a documentary crew to capture it. I had raised money from friends and acquaintances to participate. Now I questioned whether I was on the mountain for my ego, or whether I was actually ready to bow-hunt for elk. I felt as if I had let everyone involved down, including myself.

I shot four inches to the left of where I had wanted. On a large animal like an elk, that's a small margin. But a miss is a miss. The animal barely shed any blood and was running uphill rather than down. We never found the elk after hours of searching both that night and the next day.

A part of me wants to hide when I feel shame. If I hadn't had a documentary crew eager to capture all my feelings and emotions, I would have liked to disappear.

But hiding my shame is what put me in prison.

Growing up without strong masculine instruction or presence in my life, I assumed that having sex with women was what it meant to be a man. I created a story that I was shy or "unable" to have sex with women. The shame inside me grew. In my early twenties, I started to connect with women physically. But that I was still a virgin provoked shame they would eventually feel. It pushed them away and me further down the shame spiral because I kept it to myself.

In the angst and shame of going through my high school years without having sex, I committed a crime to chase after a beautiful Swiss woman. I put her on a pedestal and paid for it.

She and I never had sex. But I had already stolen the documents. Two years later, I was arrested. Over three years after that, still a virgin, and feeling more and more unworthy, I was sentenced to eight years in prison.

Throughout all those years nobody knew that I had no sexual experience. It was my deepest, darkest secret.

It wasn't until I got out of prison that I started being sexually intimate with women. When a small fling turned into my first significant heartbreak, I realized how much the shame was limiting me, and how it had directly contributed to my stealing those documents and going to prison.

In the philosophy of Carl Jung and the poet Robert Bly, the shadow-part of ourselves is what we hide, repress, or deny. The longer we keep our shadow in the dark, the more room it has to grow and aggravate. By keeping the shame around my sexuality in the dark, I was allowing that shadow to fester.

Our shadows never go away. But my goal is to keep mine in front of me. By shining a light on the shadow, I can nurture that part of me that needs nurturing and come to terms with making bad choices and decisions.

Hunting provides a unique opportunity to look at my shame. I have such a love and admiration for these animals. I want to protect and serve them. To feel that way about an animal and then to create unnecessary suffering through a missed shot brings up difficult emotions.

Now I realize that hiding or running from shame doesn't serve me. If I miss the mark in the field or in life, I must go back to the drawing board, learn the lessons, take the opportunities to grow, and process the feelings that arise. To do anything else is a disservice to myself, my loved ones, and the world.

EARTH TIME

WALKING FIFTY MILES IN A WEEK, STARING AT MY FEET methodically plodding one after another, it's easy for my steps to become measured and rhythmic. The pain of my legs and exhaustion fade into the repetition, making the experience easier to get through.

In one of these trance-like states, my hunting guide, Marc and I sought an opportunity to hunt a mule deer in the valley, giving ourselves a break from chasing elk through the mountains all day. It was a welcomed respite after nearly a week of high mileage in high altitude through rough terrain.

Pausing for a moment, Marc held his binoculars up to his face and looked at the top of a nearby mountain. Marc and I frequently stopped to "glass" the territory, using binoculars to see if we could spot an elk. Rarely did this yield anything, so I found myself lulled into a false sense of relaxation.

"I see one. He's young, and we need to move fast, but he's a good bull. We have twenty minutes to get to the top of that mountain," said Marc.

At once, I was both horrified and excited. The expectation of some rest was shattered. The mountain in front of us was about average for the range. But it felt like Everest when I considered how fast we had to move.

The sun was setting, and light was already escaping us as I nodded in agreement and followed Marc's lead. The pace was blistering. Many times, Marc had to encourage and coach me up the mountain at a pace equal to his. He was nearly fifty years old, and I was twenty-seven. How capable he was and how challenged I felt were both infuriating and inspiring.

To hunt successfully, one must set aside all desires, plans, and schedules in service of Earth time. When the sun rises and sets, when there is an animal in my path, I don't have the luxury of living on my time or indulging in what is convenient. Forced to live by the Earth's clock, I'm both humbled and appreciative.

Many of the animals I hunt are crepuscular: active around dawn and dusk. Hunting these animals means waking up before sunrise to get into the right position at dawn and hustling to do likewise before sunlight is no longer available.

Earth time is satisfying because it means *being* nature. While hunting, I can't separate myself from nature with bright blue lights and computer screens. At a deep, ancestral level, there is a feeling of "coming home" that's part connection to Earth, part humility, and part surrender.

After the twenty-minute trek to the top of the mountain, I arrived utterly exhausted, out of breath, and with my heart still beating heavily. A young bull elk walked into range forty yards up the hill. I pulled back, aimed, and shot. I was on Earth time, and this created one of the most profound hunting experiences of my life.

In those physically challenging moments, and in the countless days where Earth time forces me awake at 5:00 a.m., or doesn't let me sleep until midnight, I don't like feeling out of control. Limitations challenge and frustrate me. But in the greater scheme of things, when I reflect on the value hunting as a sacred practice has brought into my life, Earth time is one of its many gifts.

SHARING THE BURDEN

FRESH SNOW BLANKETED THE RIDGE BEFORE US, MAKING IT easier, though still not easy, to see elk in the landscape. In mid-November in Colorado, elk have already gone through months of hunting. They're extra wary, snow or not.

Nat and Chris, two men from my facilitated hunt, stood with a guide, glassing the snowy hillside, when three elk appeared. They must have been bedded down under trees to have gone unnoticed until getting up to eat.

Sensing the opportunity, a guide shouted at Nat to shoot a calf elk nearly from behind. In a moment of clarity and courage, he decided it was not the right shot for him. He waited despite the cajoling of the guide, and it paid off.

A few minutes later, another calf came into view, providing a perfect broadside shot that was a much better placement. Nat took his shot.

As the first shot hit the calf, Chris scoped it and shot his own round to ensure it died. Elk are big, and the rule of thumb is to keep shooting until the animal is dead and on the ground.

Chris reloaded and shot again. Miss. Nat reloaded and shot again. Miss.

Hitting an already wounded animal who's fleeing is no easy task. Nat tried reloading, but his gun jammed. Chris reloaded, aimed, and as he fired, a mother cow elk instinctively moved in front and effectively took a bullet for her calf.

Having already wounded a cow elk the night before, Chris was distraught. Nat, getting his gun fixed and reloaded, put the third and final shot into the already wounded calf.

Chris and Nat experienced chaos that evening. They were mindful, present, and doing their best to take not just any shot but *the right shot*. Still, the circumstances turned against them. They did not get a quick, painless kill.

We later tracked but never retrieved the cow elk. Another wounded animal. All told, six shots were fired. Despite our best efforts, we had killed one animal and wounded two. I'd never before experienced that poor ratio.

In our shared sadness the night before, I guided the men through a meditation to feel the pain of the wounded animal slowly dying in the bitter cold blizzard. We were hunting in the territory of the Ute tribe in Colorado, and I remembered a Ute proverb:

What matters who kills the game when we can all eat of it?

The corollary is also true. We all share the responsibility for wounding an animal. That's part of sharing in the hunt's collective success or failure.

We've created an unjust world if the individual must share the kill but goes unsupported when wounding or missing an animal. Hunting in this way provides a glimpse of how our ancestors once shared responsibility, not as a metaphor, but as a practice deeply embedded in our DNA.

We all face this dilemma daily. Do we share our wealth, bounty, and gifts, or hoard them for ourselves? Do we point the finger at others, claiming our own innocence, or do we share the load to ease the burden of our fellow man?

GUILT

DIRT FILLED THE DRY AIR AS A YOUNG, WOUNDED WHITE-tailed deer writhed on the ground in front of me. After receiving a spinal injury from my first arrow, his mind and instinct operated separately from his body. His legs were not functioning.

When an animal is hit in the spine, they often don't die immediately. But they can't escape, either. Watching the young deer's desperate attempt at survival was gut-wrenching.

Having experienced this once before, I quickly nocked another arrow and shot him through the chest cavity, hitting vital organs. His retching body became more violent, convulsing in myriad directions like an exorcism.

In a moment of inner turmoil, I looked away, not wanting to see the animal suffer. I quickly realized that viewing this was my inner work for the day. It was an opportunity to feel and take full responsibility for the consequences of eating meat.

When the dust settled, and the eerie silence that accompanies fresh death descended, guilt washed over me. Had

I taken a poor shot? Had I practiced too little? As I questioned myself, I asked forgiveness for the animal who had suffered through my incompetence.

Over time, I've come to realize that my guilt said more about my separation from nature than it did about the act of killing an animal. As long as I enter the woods hunting as a human feeling separate from nature, the more remorse I experience. When I feel that I am a separate entity entering a foreign land and taking something from it, guilt accompanies me. This feeling dissipates the more I feel embedded into nature. When I am *being* nature, I feel less guilt.

This does not mean feeling guilt is wrong. What often replaces this emotion is a mixture of sadness, joy, and pride. Regardless of my role and connection to nature as a human animal, it's sad to remove an animal from its family and life.

Most modern, western humans are disconnected from nature. We do not feel ourselves *being* nature. Even those who hunt have thousands of years of Judeo-Christian programming to unwind. Humans are pitted against nature and seen as taming, restricting, and imposing our will as a species upon her. Through a western lens, the world is ours for the taking. I feel that in myself as well.

One example from the hunting world will suffice. Wild hogs are disparaged for destruction of agricultural land, even though humans introduced them. In fact, they now create a variety of habitats, adding to long-term biodiversity. They spread and plant seeds and fungi much as black bears did before humans whittled down their numbers and range. One phrase that moralizes hog hunting goes: "Kill a hog, save the world." I'm doubtful that's the case, and relating to the Earth in that way sets a dangerous precedent.

Our relationship with wild hogs provides clues for how we interact with nature around us. Am I hunting for myself, for my community, for the land, for my higher power, or for the animal? Am I hunting as a part of nature rather than separate from it?

These are the questions I ask myself when I'm feeling guilty. I no longer wish to pit myself against nature as an intruder or outsider, separate from Earth.

THE KILL

VIOLENCE

CROSSING A TREE LINE, I SPOTTED THE BLACK, HAIRY BODY of a large wild hog about one hundred yards away. I immediately dropped the shooting tripod for Luke to rest his gun on. I told him that the animal was at a poor angle, but he should be prepared to take the shot as soon as it turned.

The time between our group of five crossing the tree line and Luke taking the shot was less than thirty seconds. Things moved quickly, as they often do.

The first shot rang out before I expected Luke to line up the animal. As it hit, the hog started yelling and squealing, a sound none of the men on that trip will forget.

I told Luke to reload quickly and fire again. It seemed the shot went directly into the ground. I assumed that Luke's adrenaline was pumping and, after the pig started moving, he would have a hard time hitting it a second time.

I told Luke to put his gun on safe as I took out my knife. The hog is still squealing and bellowing in pain. The men look my way for leadership. By now, I'm on a mission, running to the animal, bounding between rocks, shedding my backpack, dropping items in my pockets to move unencumbered.

When I arrive, the pig is gasping for breath and on his way out. At this point, I'm near the animal ready to stab it, but also respectful of the strength, power, and aggression of his final moments. I pause and watch him die.

The rifle fire, the squealing, the mad dash to plunge a knife into the animal, and the animal's own aggression are all reminders of the violence in our lives on Earth.

Our existence on this planet, especially in civilization's present form, is paved with violence. Whether it is the coercion and abuse of people in faraway countries or the animals, trees, plants, and insects we're killing off in droves, we are all perpetrators.

There is no diet or modern consumer culture free from violence. To eat mass-produced vegetable crops is violent to the soil's microbiome, to the insects, to the baby fawns caught in a combine tractor, and to the mice poisoned in the silo.

I speak of food because that is a central theme at the heart of hunting and my life—all our lives. Violence goes beyond our food, encompassing our consumption and actions.

A twenty-dollar oak stool from IKEA is that low price only because of illegal logging in Siberia, destroying the habitat of the largest and most charismatic big cat in the world, the Amur tiger.

The plastic we buy that ends up in ocean mammals and fish is violence. A life free from violence is an illusion.

There are only a few ways of processing this violence. Some will choose to turn the other way. The violence is too painful to look at. I've been there and empathize. Some will cynically relish taking as much for themselves as possible. Others will take responsibility for their violence whenever and wherever they can.

Taking responsibility for the violence connected to the meat I eat feels right, especially when the animal looks and feels a lot like me. I have shot or stabbed many animals, often at close range, sometimes petting their heads and whispering last words as they pass.

Much of the experience is violent. Regardless of how "natural" it is for a predator to kill prey, that does not make it any less violent, or the violence any less saddening.

But taking responsibility for our violence is the only answer where violence is the law of the land. The deeper our emotional links to the acts we perpetrate, the more we can connect with our decisions. I won't waste the meat that I've killed myself, and this is taking responsibility for my violence.

Many people outsource their violence at the collective level. The meat they eat comes from animals they've never met and slaughterhouses they've never seen, managed by people they don't know.

Before hunting, I thought of meat in terms of grocery stores and restaurants. The thought that I could take responsibility for what I eat occurred only in adulthood.

What's sinister about outsourcing our violence is that violence is more harmful when it's consolidated in the hands of the few.

When the multinational, multibillion-dollar Tyson Foods and Cargills of the world monopolize violence, they create factory farms. The legs of chickens injected with steroids break under the weight of their own girth, and they spend the rest of their short lives sitting in a pile of their own excrement.

When violence is distributed throughout the system, it's less harmful.

Every man, woman, and child of the Hadza people in Tanzania knows how to hunt and kill animals. The necklace I often wear is a baboon tooth taken from an animal they hunted. I witnessed great violence watching them hunt the baboon with emaciated dogs, shooting it with arrows, and then beating the dogs to ensure only humans could eat the meat. Violence is part of their way of life, their culture, and their being, but at least they take responsibility for it.

PAIN

LATE SPRING IN THE TEXAS HILL COUNTRY CAN BE AS HOT as the blistering summer. The mornings may feel cool and enjoyable, but afternoon quickly turns into searing heat. It was in this environment that I first used kambo, a toxic frog secretion from South America that indigenous people have used for thousands of years for both hunting and healing.

For tribes in the Amazon, one purpose of kambo is to increase sensory perception, visual acuity, and the capacity to hunt. For me, it was my first experience of using a mind-altering substance derived from an animal rather than a plant or fungus. I took the opportunity of connecting with the animal kingdom with the intention of experiencing what it felt like to be hunted.

Because kambo is a toxin the giant monkey frog uses to immobilize and keep predators away, it is often a painful and literally gut-wrenching experience. It felt like my insides were being wrung out like a wet rag. Then it felt like a knife penetrating my organs. In those moments of pain, I could experience glimpses of what my prey might have felt when being struck with an arrow.

As the steady drum beat and ceremonial singing went on around me, I dry heaved and cried. Somewhere I let go of my reality and surrendered to death, if that was to overtake me. Passing from this life felt okay if the pain would just stop.

The animals I fish and hunt feel pain. Fish have pain receptors around their mouth, and their hindbrain registers similar sensations to humans when caught with a hook.

Wild hogs know which animals they are related to and groom and play together. I've seen antelope and deer react to one of their loved ones dying in front of them. They smell and investigate their passed friend, sister, mother. They keep their heads lowered and move with somber slowness.

I must accept that I experience physical and emotional pain and inflict it on others. I have a choice whether to lean into the pain fully and embrace and pass through it, or deny, resist, and suppress it.

The reason I surrendered to death in my kambo experience wasn't because of the pain of the toxin itself. It was because of the pain of losing my partner of many years and finding out, just one week before, that she was with another man. It was an emotional, gut-wrenching pain replete with shame and sadness. It's the pain of being "not enough" I have felt since then and will feel again.

But pain is a signal and catalyst for growing. Indigenous people have known and practiced this for ages. John Lame Deer, a Lakota Sioux medicine man, said, "We believe it is up to every one of us to help each other, even through the pain of our bodies. Pain to us is not 'abstract,' but very real. We do not lay this burden onto our god, nor do we want to miss being face to face with the spirit power."

During a group hunt that I led, a participant named David came with the intention of having a quick, clean kill. Amid a chaotic environment on the hunt, he shot an animal in the guts, wounding it. I walked the group, saddened by this pain, through a guided meditation.

We put our attention on our stomachs, envisioning a suffering hog struggling for life in the shade. An animal wounded, especially in the guts, will die a slow, painful death from infection if they do not bleed out first. This reality dawned on David, and he began to cry. I consoled him through his pain, acknowledging the pain of the animal, and using the pain as a catalyst for the entire group's growth.

I'm grateful for this experience and that of kambo, which has shaped my view of the pain that animals experience. With added respect, I practice more thoroughly. I'm more patient, and I take the right shot. I've learned from my own pain to empathize and ease others' pain. This is the relationship with pain I want to maintain in hunting and in life.

RESPONSIBILITY

WATER DROPLETS SPORADICALLY MOISTENED THE FALL leaves, rendering the ordinary crunching sound they make inaudible. Deer had likely walked around my blind without my hearing their footsteps. My attention was fixed in front of me, where a network of trails crisscrossed the landscape. This is where my first opportunity would come.

A male, white-tailed deer no more than two years old slowly made his way towards me, picking his favorite leaves off a low-hanging branch. I was surprised the deer was so interested in the leaves when live-oak acorns were already covering the ground. Mating season had started, and bucks were coming through the twenty-five-acre property I was hunting.

As the deer moved slowly, I could feel the anticipation rising in my body. Now directly in front of me, this young buck gave me a great shooting opportunity. His head was tilted up, taking leaves from a branch, and he was standing broadside, exposing his entire flank and organs. As I pulled my arrow back, he was too preoccupied with his food to notice the compound bow's slight squeak as I released.

The arrow hit the target but deflected off his ribs into his spine. The animal went down. He tried to crawl away, but his front legs weren't working. In my beginner mind, I had messed up. Any suffering that didn't result in a quick death was a disaster.

I nocked another arrow and shot, but he was writhing and flailing so vigorously that I missed him completely. I aimed another but really had no shot. Panic seeped into my bloodstream, my mind froze, and my body tingled. I didn't know what to do. This was only the second animal I had ever killed. I felt lost and poorly prepared.

Eventually, I realized the best way to finish killing the animal was with a knife. In my naiveté, I walked up close, something nobody should do when a wounded, antlered male is thrashing a body weighing over a hundred pounds.

Reaching out my hand, keeping my head and vital organs as far away as possible, I grabbed his antlers to keep his head anchored in place. With my left hand, I slipped my knife under his shoulder and into his heart.

I remember looking at him in the eyes, his mouth open and tongue agape. His gaze spoke of betrayal and fear. He made no noise but didn't need to. I could sense his struggle and feel the heaviness of the moment. I whispered, "I'm sorry, I'm so sorry," feeling guilty about what I believed was an improper shot.

Once his life had passed and I settled in, the post-kill quietness fell over me. My environment became heightened and surreal. The mist and occasional droplet were among the only things that moved. After some time recovering emotionally, I got to work.

This animal was the first that I had killed solely with my own skill and capacity. Instead of working with a guide at a hunting property, I had to decide the best course of action myself. Now was the first time I needed to gut and dress an animal as well.

The gravity of gutting the animal hit me. I was rankled with self-doubt and remember calling at least two friends, asking if they were around to help, but they weren't. I found some YouTube tutorial videos as a refresher and slowly went to work.

The meat from that hunt was some of the most rewarding I've ever had. I had worked hard and taken the responsibility of doing everything on my own.

For myself and many of the men I facilitate Sacred Hunting rites of passage for, taking responsibility for the meat we eat is a primary motivator to hunt. The masculine is drawn to responsibility, to shoulder a burden and make meaning from it.

Jordan Peterson once said, "The purpose of life is finding the largest burden that you can bear and bearing it." I eat meat. The largest burden for a meat eater is to hunt and kill an animal. I shoulder that responsibility, which is among the most meaningful commitments in my life.

busy, busy, busy bees
these humans are such mysteries
floating around, never knowing what they want
so go forth, go for with your morning, dear
with the sun's arms on your back and the love that you left behind

TRAUMA

WHEN AN ARROW PASSES THROUGH THE LUNGS, THE BLOOD that leaves an animal's body is foamy, almost like soap lathering during a bath. The lungs fill with blood and, if the arrow hits both lungs, the animal dies relatively quickly.

After my first shot penetrated Alice, a large female bison, with a "pop," I knew the placement was good. When I saw the bubbling blood, this was confirmed.

The first shot would kill Alice, but her size meant that the time before she died would be longer than with the deer or hogs I'd hunted. I wanted to end her suffering as quickly as possible.

Following the blood trail led me to her in less than a minute. She was upset, confused, and determined to survive. I prepared another arrow, drew back the bow, and shot. The angle was such that her huge and powerful ribs deflected the small, carbon-fiber arrow, even though it was moving faster than 300 feet per second.

I ran after her again and took another shot. This time I was feeling the chase, the nerves, and the emotions. I pulled the shot a few inches onto her meaty shoulder. No vitals were hit, and she was greatly irritated.

I remember dropping to one knee, emotionally exhausted from watching her suffer and struggle, even though the time had been short. In these early hunting days, I was less patient and more frantic to have her die without suffering than I would later become.

I asked my guide to put a final bullet in her head, ending her suffering. From down on my knee, I looked at her, feeling her power, her will to survive, her obstinacy. She had a lot of strength and I just begged her to go down. Tears were welling up in my eyes, and the long, drawn-out death felt like suffering that I had created.

There was relief when she was finally dead. Tension was released, and I could now soothe my guilt about the first shot not going straight into the heart and killing her instantly.

Over the three hours of gutting, butchering, and processing the animal, I felt gratitude and appreciation for how much meat she was providing. Her fur was soft and organs enormous. I took her tongue last, having almost forgotten that it is one of the animal's most prized cuts.

As I drove home with three, 150-quart coolers filled with meat, I listened to one of my favorite musicians, Nahko

Bear, singing his song "Alice." It felt like the song was for the bison I had just hunted. I started crying, all the emotions of gratitude, sadness, guilt, and joy coming up along with the beautiful piano playing. In that moment, I named the bison Alice. Her skull adorns my walls, and her hide lies on my bed.

For many months afterward, I would look at the skull or fur and feel a twisting sensation near my heart. There was a visceral sensation each time I remembered killing Alice.

A friend experienced in such matters said that physical discomfort is a telltale sign of emotional trauma. Killing Alice had left some lasting trauma in my body.

I resisted this, even though I intuitively knew it to be true. I found so much goodness in the practice of hunting, I did not want it to be a source of trauma, but it was.

All of us have trauma from our childhood, from our intimate relationships, from our friendships, from life. Sometimes we recognize that the trauma comes from relationships that are unhealthy for us. Sometimes the trauma is nobody's fault, but the result of circumstances that cause us to hold on.

One participant hunted for the first time with me to reclaim, connect with, and integrate the killer archetype. He was a member of the Israeli Defense Force special forces, a group that kidnapped and killed enemies of the state. When he was a young man, his profession had him kill people, sometimes innocents. He had done much contemplation and inner work to heal the trauma, but this is what he brought to the hunt.

As researcher Dr. Bessel van der Kolk once wrote, "The body keeps the score." Our body stores and holds trauma until we work through it at our own pace and with our own tools.

Sometimes I resist trauma, as I did with the bison Alice and the pain associated with hunting her. When I resist such trauma, it persists and grows.

However, my gold is when I see the trauma for what it is and learn to transmute it. Instead of experiencing the "Alice trauma" as a sign that I'm bad or wrong, it led me to realize that killing another animal is a sacred and intimate act.

This trauma informs the care with which I undertake both my hunting practice and facilitating the experience for others. It creates immense gratitude and appreciation for every meal. My hunting practice reminds me that trauma is part of life and that healing and turning trauma into wisdom for others is its hidden gift.

CROSSING OVER

If you die before you die, you won't die when you die.
—St. Paul the Apostle

If there is a particularly emotionally and physically tense moment on a hunt, it's drawing back the bow with the intent of shooting a nearby animal. Sometimes, the moment is tense because the animal has not provided a clear opportunity, and it's the hunter's role to wait, patient and steadfast. Sometimes it's tense because the animal provides a perfect shooting opportunity, and taking the shot quickly and effectively has become a priority.

On rare occasions, the tension comes from a broken or defective bow. One crisp, spring morning, my compound bow's release—its trigger—broke, sending an arrow careening into the bushes rather than the mountain sheep twenty-five yards in front of me. After hours of practice, driving, and hiking, my bow failed me the moment when it mattered most.

Before giving up, the local hunting guide and I pondered solutions to our current predicament. It was my equipment and my fault, but he astutely realized his customer hadn't had the experience he had wanted. As with many solutions on the hunt, we found an imperfect fix that included barbed wire.

We quietly stalked backwards to avoid spooking the animals. It was not long before we found a fence of barbed wire meant for keeping cattle off the property. In a stroke of backwoods genius, my guide found a loose piece, wrapped it around my broken release, and told me to try the bow again. It worked.

It took no more than thirty minutes before we were searching for the herd of sheep with newfound excitement and resolve. It wasn't long before we found them.

The crosswind was in our favor, and the animals were looking into the sun. Hunched over, making myself as small as possible, I walked gingerly to a large agarita bush less than twenty yards from the animals. This spiny plant native to central Texas bloomed with beautiful red berries and yellow flowers. But it also had strong boundaries and gave me a poke.

With the agarita and crosswind providing me strong cover, I was able to bide my time, pick my target, and wait. Drawing an eighty-pound compound bow back is not too difficult, but holding it for longer than a minute can be. My arms started to ache and cramp, and the blood in my head pounded deeper and fuller.

Turning and looking at me, the sheep almost seemed to offer himself to my arrow. Friends who later saw the video of the hunt would say he seemed to have a betrayed look on his face. Certainly, the sheep was confused about what I was and my role in his life. But the arrow I shot was true to its mark. It passed completely through the animal's chest cavity and lodged itself in a cactus pad behind him.

What happened next was a common occurrence for anyone sensitive to the feelings and emotions of living creatures. I was sad seeing the animal gallop fifteen yards and slow down. I was afraid my shot was not as perfect as it seemed. I thought I might shoot another arrow through his chest to kill him more quickly and humanely.

I decided to wait, something I rarely did. At first, it was because the sheep was sitting in a prone position on the ground, giving me no real shooting opportunity. Then, it was to witness the quasi-psychedelic state the sheep seemed to be in transferring from our Earthly realm to the next.

It was strangely peaceful to see the sheep drift out of his body, his head rolled and mouth agape. One could imagine he was in pain or suffering, but in that moment, it felt more like a trance.

There is no single moment when I saw him die. The process lasted a few minutes as we waited patiently, silently, feeling the spirits of the dead in the calm of nature.

Every hunter knows the silence and stillness that accompanies the passing of an animal. The death may be violent, even electric, but when all is done, there's a profound tranquility.

What happens on the other side of death is anyone's guess. As a hunter, I deal out death by bow and arrow. All I can imagine is the reflection of the experience before me. It seems more peaceful and certainly less awful than we make death out to be in our own lives.

Attacked and nearing death, Scottish explorer, David Livingstone, provides some insight into the experience. In 1844, leading an expedition into Africa, he came upon a lion and fired, injuring but not crippling it. Before Livingstone could reload, the lion set upon him, wounding him in the arm and breaking bone. Livingstone would have died had it not been for his companions.

When asked about his experience, Livingstone recalled a dreamy state with no pain or terror. He was conscious of what was happening, but did not have the fretful, chaotic experience we westerners project onto dying.

As a society, we are removed and disconnected from death. Most people never experience the death of an animal while putting food on their plates. We rarely experience death. With so little connection to the reality of the cycle of life and death, it's no wonder many fear the displacement from our earthly body into the unknown realm that follows.

My hunting is a consistent practice and meditation on death. I witness death, walk animals through their process of dying—sometimes with kind words and petting their bodies. I witness the death I create with each meal consuming their flesh. This practice reminds me of my own mortality, that I too will sometime pass, and I hope to provide nutrients to Earth as so many animals have done for me. I kill and I practice my death.

HONORING THE DEAD

INTIMACY

PART OF HONORING THE DEAD IS HONORING THE INTIMACY of its soul merging with ours. This takes place over many months as my friends, family, and I consume the animal. But it's also present when they look up at me after an intense moment of connection, perhaps after I stab them in the heart.

In these intimate and tender moments, jokes and humor evaporate. Just as making jokes after an emotional sexual experience is off-putting, there is a certain seriousness that accompanies me on hunting trips and particularly in those moments. This is not to *perform* seriousness. Rather, I feel the reality of the intimate act I'm partaking in.

Many of the animals I kill have names: Alice, Lupe, Ren. These come to me later, a mix of the moment in time, the experience of the hunt, and the behavior I witnessed.

Naming the animals is one way to avoid objectifying them as "meat to fill the freezer." It's true they provide meat, and I'm sincerely grateful for that. But it's also true that this was a son, daughter, sister, brother, father, mother. In naming an animal, I remember it was an integral and loved member of a family and want to *feel* the truth of that perspective.

Each man who participates in a facilitated hunting experience has an opportunity to develop this intimacy. On the first day, I instruct men to write a love letter to the animal he will be hunting.

All men have some experience with love letters, and this creates a close connection with the animal. One man recounted expressing admiration for the animal as a mother, understanding what motherhood looks like from the example of his wife and child. When we see the animal akin to our wife and child, we cannot help but feel intimate with them.

By writing a letter, we personify the animal and acknowledge our similarities, much like our ancestors would have. As John Vaillant says, "For hunting societies, animals were not seen as food. They were seen as blood relatives, spiritual companions, hunting guides, and sources of power and connection to the surrounding world."

My capacity to appreciate the intimacy of killing and consuming another animal transfers to other aspects of my life. I feel an intimacy with all my environment—the trees, birds, and insects. This adds a richness and vibrancy to my life and increases my capacity for intimacy within myself and with the people closest to me.

The men who write the love letters to animals they kill often find it to be a profound part of the practice. Sometimes, as in the case of Matt, participants also write a letter to the animal afterwards:

Frederick, or as I've begun to call you, Freddy,

I admire your strength.

Your broken horn, and the fact that you held on for as long as you did shows me how strong you are. How much fight was in you.

I have a lot of fight in me too, and now I get to carry some of yours in me forever.

I'm sorry for the slow, violent, nature of your death. I promise next time I will do everything I can to be more precise.

I don't know if you had a family, but I'm sure there's someone you care about.

To them, I also apologize.

I'm sure there's someone you left behind who cares about you. I know this, because I care about you.

I don't know the details of your life, and you don't know the details of mine, but we are forever connected.

Finally, I want you to know that I deeply wish you didn't die scared. I know you did, but that in no way takes away from your strength.

You are a warrior.

I will never remember you as anything less.

With Love, Matt

NO WASTE

...the characteristics of a bird or an animal were desired by the Indians who, in some cases, wore a part of the bird or animal on their persons; the deer, because the animal can endure thirst a long time; the hawk as the surest bird of prey; the elk in gallantry; the frog in watchfulness; the owl in night-wisdom and gentle ways; the bear, which though fierce, has given many medicinal herbs for the good of man; the kit-fox, which is active and wily; the crow, which is especially direct as well as swift in flight; and the wolf, in hardihood.
—Frances Densmore

"Ask the winged beings for permission," said Star Heart. He meant that I should ask for guidance in a dream state, a common practice for spiritual and visionary insight.

In the early morning hours between 3:00 and 4:00 a.m., there is a hazy, half-awake state between waking consciousness and the spirit realm. This time of night is often associated with rapid eye movement (REM) sleep, when dimethyltryptamine (DMT) is present in our brains. If you are awake during this time, you can ask spiritual questions in a fashion similar to how you might ask them of the ayahuasca vine or other plant medicines.

I was instructed to ask the spirit of the grouse for permission to use six feet I had saved from a hunt to make a necklace, a hunting totem to be worn only during that sacred time.

> *Me: Can I use grouse feet to make my necklace?*

In response, I heard a raven caw three times and saw an owl.

The answer was too cryptic to know whether I had the winged beings' blessing. But having birds depicted vividly in my vision surprised me. It seemed that asking spirits questions during the dream state could work if I was in tune with myself.

Two nights later, I asked again.

> *Me: "Can I use the grouse feet to make my necklace? To have the winged creature's spirit with me on the hunt?"*
>
> *Answer: "Step into the medicine."*
>
> *Me: "Do I have full permission?"*
>
> *Answer: "Yes. You do."*

The answer flashed vividly in my mind as clearly as ayahuasca visions I've had. I then worked with Star Heart to create a necklace of grouse feet to be used when hunting.

In my home, I have feathers that I picked up from a bird who had been hit by the side of the road. I have skulls and hides adorning my bed and walls. Deer-hoof rattles accompany me on hunting trips.

This is all part of my process of honoring as much of the animal as possible. If I'm going to kill an animal, I want to respect it by using and keeping as much as I can.

Sometimes there's a practical purpose involved. The Timacula tribe of Florida were said to hunt deer by wearing deerskins to conceal themselves. There are stories of Plains tribes, before the advent of horses, using coyote skins to get close to the bison they were hunting.

Sometimes honoring these animal parts has more spiritual overtones. The rabbit's foot, which is supposed to bring good luck, derives this power from the animal's capacity to avoid predators with speed and agility. A rabbit's foot brings the animal's characteristics, traits, and values into daily life.

I have a baboon-tooth necklace that reflects my fierce protectiveness and loyalty. It reminds me never to forget how important my people are to me. It's an amulet or totem made from teeth that would have otherwise been discarded somewhere in Tanzania.

It's not possible for me to use every last bit of the animal. There are organs I can't eat, perhaps because we have lost touch with the ways in which our indigenous ancestors may have done so.

Nothing goes to waste in the animal kingdom. Earth will reclaim all the parts of an animal I don't take with me. She will reclaim bone and sinew, feeding it to the vultures, coyotes, and insects. When I see roadkill or the wanton, egotistical slaughter of animals, I take some solace in the fact that, in nature, nothing goes to waste.

The motivations behind my decisions about which parts I save and which I don't are critical. Am I choosing to leave something on the land after a kill because I'm being lazy, selfish, or absent-minded? Or am I choosing to leave it because I realize I can't eat it, but wild creatures can?

The practice of understanding my motivations and intentions involves intuition and feeling. Only I have the awareness to know if I am living in accordance with my values or not. To fully honor and respect the animal, I must, to the best of my ability, leave no waste. Sometimes this means taking parts I can't eat, but others will.

It's even more important to fully embrace all the hunt's lessons and wisdom. I do my best to practice what I teach others: to take each hunting experience seriously and to learn and grow as a man.

These lessons nourish both my body and soul. I scrape the animal's bone so I can be in the right relationship with myself, my community, and my greater mission.

Even after the meat is gone and nothing physical remains, if we retain the memories that guide us to greater capabilities, we are honoring the animal to the utmost.

RETURN

By the same power that slays you, I am too slain; and I too shall be consumed. For the law that delivered you into my hand shall deliver me into a mightier hand. Your blood and my blood is naught but the sap that feeds the tree of heaven.
—Kahlil Gibran

LIKE MANY OF THE ANIMALS I HUNT, I'M A CREATURE OF habit. Often, I walk the same path or route simply because I'm used to it. The habit offers comfort.

One morning on my routine walk, I found a dead snake on the path. It was a rat snake, much larger than the Texas hognose snake I nurture as a pet.

Because it sheds its skin, in many indigenous cultures, the snake is a sign of transition. It's customary in my belief system to pay careful, reverent homage to all creatures living and dead. I sang a transition song for the snake, picked it up by one side, and placed it in a grassy area filled with brush.

Over the next few days, I experienced the snake slowly return to the Earth. The meat thinned, the skin withered, and all around the dead animal were ants and other small bugs taking back its nutrients. My habitual walking pattern became a time-lapse of the awesome splendor of nature recycling nutrients back into herself.

Since the time I started hunting and pondering death more seriously, I've felt excited and joyful to have my body returned to the Earth like this snake. The idea of cremation, turning the nutrients in my body into heat, and letting my ashes dissipate without serving nature, seems foreign and untrue for me. Being buried deep in the ground in clothing far from animals also seems strange and unnatural.

When I die, the (currently illegal) way I'd like to be returned to Earth is by being propped up against a tree and letting animals receive nutrition from my body, as I have received it from theirs.

This is not such a strange request. For most of human history, indigenous peoples performed "sky burials" to return loved ones to Earth. These varied by culture, but often involved placing the corpse on a platform to be eaten by birds and other animals.

To return our bodies to the land is to be a part of the land. It's a release into the unknown and our final act of service to the planet that has nourished and supported our lives.

In regions of the Amazonian jungle, tribespeople use eye

drops called *Sananga* to help hunt in the black of night. While it is painful to the eyes, it also enhances vision and is used ceremonially for emotional release and clearing the dark energies known as "panema."

In one of my facilitated experiences, Sananga eye drops were applied to the eyes of men lying down in a small, rocky outcropping. Bryan, one of the attendees, turned to me, hugged me, and started to cry.

Only moments before, a small bird had perched particularly near us. Bryan's young daughter, who had passed away a couple years before, shows up for him as birds. He was thinking about her as the bird landed near us, and for him, it was a sign that she had returned.

This was Bryan's medicine for the weekend. It was profound for him to be able to process the passing of his child through the "death medicine" that manifests in a hunting experience.

On the final hunt, Bryan had an opportunity to pull the trigger and kill an animal. In reflection, he realized that none of his intentions for being on that land included him doing this. He had accomplished everything he set out to achieve on that trip and was content to sit with those lessons and help other men butcher and skin the animal. He reveled in the process and the collective sharing of the meat over a meal.

FOR THE COLLECTIVE

SERVICE

ON A SUNNY, DECEMBER MORNING, JEREMY TAKES OFF THE hood from the head of a peregrine falcon on his arm. The bird leaps into the air. On command, she gains altitude and begins circling and awaiting prey. We are participating in a four-thousand-year-old tradition called falconry, the hunting of wild game in partnership with a bird of prey.

As the bird circles above us, Jeremy and I walk with a dog toward a small pond with a few ducks on the surface. The dog runs at the pond, scaring the ducks off the water, and the falcon spots an opportunity. Starting from high in the air, she tucks in her wings and uses gravity and aerodynamics to become a heat-seeking missile targeting an airborne duck. We hear an incredibly loud thud: the first of the season.

We run to the duck and falcon, who is proudly covering her prey. My guide has provided her a great opportunity, and she's succeeded with her end of the bargain. This is one of the few human relationships with animals that is a genuine partnership. The bird could fly away at any moment, deciding it could do better without a human support system. If the relationship is mutual, and I'm showing up to support the bird, she remains. This partnership with an Earth being is what draws me to falconry.

I envision a relationship with land also motivated by partnership and service. I see the forest bringing forth birds, bees, and bugs. I see a deer eating figs on the ground. I see the goose eggs we've offered as gifts to the snakes.

More important than what I see in this vision is what I *feel*. In my body I *feel* an appreciation of the Earth, I *feel* the honor to serve some small portion of it, and I *feel* a purity of respect and devotion to the planet that gives us all life.

I'm thankful for visions like this, aided by plants like ayahuasca. They allow me to reach places in myself that I'm unable to reach without their help. The feelings of love, awe, virtue, and beauty that pure service to Earth evokes are visceral memories that follow me in my life.

These peak experiences are motivating and inspiring. But, like any peak experience, it's up to me to enact and embody those virtues in my ordinary waking consciousness and daily existence.

Hunting and eating the meat I kill allows me to embody service to both the animal and the land. Sharing that meat with others allows me to embody service to my community.

Serving meat that I have hunted extends the animal's gift. She will live on not only through me, but through all my friends. At the table, the animal will bring all of us closer together emotionally. She also brings us closer physically, because our bodies will turn her flesh into our own. In some instances, pregnant women will turn this animal's death into new life.

Service is not purely for those who are served. When I give of myself, I feel a sense of great pride. I feel confident that I have been successful on the hunt or in my life, and that I can be of service with my time, resources, and energy.

DEFEND THE SACRED

*We have to believe in a more beautiful world
in order to serve it.*
—Charles Eisenstein

DURING THE RAINY SEASON, HUMIDITY MAKES THE SEARING Texas heat all the more challenging. Seven men sat under shade trees and among the bushes, while two guardians, the term I use for my co-support brethren during Sacred Hunting experiences, circled the outskirts of our outdoor ceremony space.

On plant medicine, in the heat, with everyone running low on water, it was particularly powerful to have a water blessing to close the ceremony. I opened a Mason jar filled with natural spring water from Barton Springs, an important watering hole for many indigenous people, including the Comanche. This living water traveled with me over four hours to west Texas, and we took a moment to feel gratitude and pay our respects. Life depends on water, and to take a moment to reflect on that out in nature and the elements felt potent.

As we silently contemplated the water, I felt the collective carelessness of our relationship to this precious resource. I thought of the DuPont chemical conglomerate that knowingly poisoned the drinking water of tens of thousands of people in West Virginia. I thought of the oil spills in Alaska and the Gulf of Mexico, seeing pelicans covered in oil and unable to move. I cried, reflecting on the way we have failed water on Earth. We're connected with all beings, and to poison our water is to poison ourselves. In fact, the chemicals found in waterways are also found in humans.

Before my relationship with hunting, I didn't have a sense of injustice and grief about the way we humans treat Earth. It's certainly not only myself who has awakened to the role humans must play in defending our ecosystems.

In 1884, heartbroken and politically disgraced, Theodore Roosevelt retreated as far from his New York City upbringing as he could possibly go. Two days after giving birth to a daughter, his wife died. That year's presidential election was so challenging that he retired and set out to North Dakota.

Roosevelt was a city boy without much outdoor experience, certainly not as a cowboy or hunter in the American West. Over many years, he participated in hunting excursions that healed him after his loss, connected him to the land, and laid the groundwork for one of America's greatest conservationists. Roosevelt oversaw the preservation of at least 230 million acres by many means necessary. He valued and defended nature.

We may be too late to save our species on Earth, but she will be fine in the long arc of time, with or without us. How we relate to her at this pivotal juncture is a reflection of how we relate to ourselves.

By seeing Earth as a living being, a mother worthy of love, respect, and admiration, I feel a devotion to her that transcends everything else in my life. She is always giving, asking nothing in return. She can be harsh, but she is always fair. She is part of us, and we are part of her. May we all find the relationship to her that enables us to stand and defend what is sacred.

Made in the USA
Columbia, SC
17 August 2023